AN INTRODUCTION TO THE MULTINATIONALS

Also by Michel Ghertman

EUROPEAN RESEARCH IN INTERNATIONAL
BUSINESS *(with James Leontiades)*
LA PRISE DE DÉCISION
GESTION INTERNATIONALE DE L'ENTREPRISE
(with others)

Also by Margaret Allen

THE MONEY BOOK: Your Money and Your Life
SELLING DREAMS
THE PAN GUIDE TO INSURANCE
THE BLACK ECONOMY *(with Arnold Heertje and Harry
Cohen)*

AN
INTRODUCTION
TO THE
MULTINATIONALS

Michel Ghertman and Margaret Allen

St. Martin's Press   New York

Originally written in French by Michel Ghertman
as *Les Multinationales* (Presses Universitaires de France, Paris, 1982)
Translated into English by Christina Laporte
The translation was rewritten and revised by
Margaret Allen under the direction of
Michel Ghertman

All rights reserved. For information, write:
St. Martin's Press, Inc., 175 Fifth Avenue, New York, NY 10010
Printed in Great Britain
Published in the United Kingdom by The Macmillan Press Ltd for
Institute for Research and Information on Multinationals,
45–47 Rue de Lausanne, 1201 Geneva
First published in the United States of America in 1984

ISBN 0–312–43304–2

Library of Congress Cataloging in Publication Data
Ghertman, Michel.
An introduction to the multinationals.
Translation of: Les multinationales.
Bibliography: p.
Includes index.
1. International business enterprises. I. Allen,
Margaret,   –   . II. Title.
HD2755.5.G4813   1984   338.8′8   83–22919
ISBN 0–312–43304–2

Contents

Introduction

I hope that the reader will leave behind the universal attitude which confuses fact and value, wish and reality. If we say that Dillinger's gang in a certain situation is stronger than Al Capone's, that means neither that we admire the first nor pity the second.

C. Castoriadis, *On War*, Paris:
Fayard (Coll. 'Les réalités'), 1981.

The public, academics and politicians look at multinational companies in a variety of radically different ways. To some, multinationals, with their influence linked to the power of money, consolidate the power and riches of a few to the detriment of the majority. Those with such views may even go so far to allege that multinationals are able to manipulate or overthrow foreign governments. Others, in contrast, regard multinationals as the most modern and efficient form of company organization and, therefore, indispensable, beneficial vehicles for economic and social progress.

In 1974, a survey[1] showed that in general, the image of multinationals is much more negative than positive: they are modern monsters, uncontrollable organisms with many tentacles.

The images are strong and concise, dominated by an impression of power and hidden activity, which are two versions of the same fear. They arouse many strong feelings, including those of a cold hybrid monster and secret, nefarious acts. All these associations are metaphors

1

for something monstrous or abnormal; the image most often evoked is that of highly complex organisms reaching out farther and farther to grab (monsters 'with antennae', octopuses 'with tentacles', 'multi-headed' hydras). Another frequent image is that of an enticer (which 'devours', 'sucks', 'swallows' or 'gulps'). We also find metaphors of obscurity – something which functions 'in the shadows', surrounded with mystery . . .[2]

Are such assertions exact, or, on the contrary, are they stereotypes? This is obviously one of the major questions which this book will seek to answer. Before so doing, however, it is necessary first of all to define what multinationals are, understand the history of their development, and analyse their functions and economic, political, social and cultural role in society today.

The definition of a multinational company throughout this book is 'any company originating in one country and having continuous activities under its control in at least two other countries, that is, foreign countries, which provide more than ten per cent of total group turnover'.[3] The company in the country of origin is generally known as the parent company, or sometimes the Head Office and the extensions into the host countries as foreign subsidiaries. The latter may be under the former's financial control (that is, majority shareowner-ship), managerial control (through a management contract), or technological control (through the transfer of technology). The definition covers both industrial and commercial firms and, increasingly, services like banks, advertising agencies and consulting and engineering companies. A multinational is not necessarily a company in the private sector of industry like Shell Transport & Trading, B.A.T. Industries, Barclays Bank or General Motors of America; it may belong to the State. Examples of the latter are British Leyland and Cable British Airways in Britain, Renault or Elf-Erap in France, or Tungsram, the Hungarian multinational. Again, a multina-tional is not necessarily a large firm: there are many small and medium-sized multinationals.[4]

Until today, the various definitions of multinational companies[5] have revealed only a part of the full range of their activities, since they have dealt solely with large industrial firms. They left aside the service industries even though more and more of the multinationals' economic activity involves services, which are, therefore, increasingly typical of the multinational phenomenon.

Depending on different authors, companies with foreign subsidiaries may be called multinationals, plurinationals, large interterritorial units, conationals, supranationals, or transnationals, but these differences in vocabulary are not particularly important. In this book the original term of multinational enterprise or company, which is widespread in a majority of university milieux throughout the world, will be used.

It is necessary, however, to mention the United Nations, as well as the different agencies attached to it, and the many researchers in Latin America, who since 1974 have systematically used the term 'transnational' to designate the very large multinationals originating in industrialized countries. This is a political choice and excludes the small and medium-sized multinational firms and all the multinationals, including some very large ones, where the parent company is in Eastern Europe or the developing countries.[6]

The transfer of technology is a form of multinationalization which is becoming increasingly important.[7] For example, a British building contractor or property developer with no subsidiaries abroad may well make a large proportion of its turnover through technology transfer outside Britain. Such transfers are complex and made up of complementary elements including plans for the construction of factories, roads, dams, hospitals or schools; furnishing equipment and materials for the particular development; training of local labour (staff and workers); getting equipment to the right place at the right time, supplying parts and maintenance. The ultimate form of transfer, and the one that best illustrates its success, is the ability of the seller to transfer to the buyer the possibility of itself creating new technology and having the means to do so. The term external transfer of technology is used when a company, which is already a multinational, or which becomes a multinational at that time, transfers technology to an indigenous firm of a country where it was not previously present. In contrast, an internal transfer occurs when the parent company transfers technology to its subsidiaries.

Such transfer activities are essential for the survival and success of the company. They demand a great deal of effort by the firm's general management and its top-level engineers and technicians.[8]

In contrast to the multinational, the company which has activities limited to a single country should be referred to as uninational, or mononational. These terms are not generally in use in the United Kingdom, but are preferable to others.[9] In particular, the term 'national company' must be avoided as it is most often used to designate state-controlled firms which have been created, or nationalized by the State. A number of these firms, however, may be multinationals. This is particularly true in France. Thus there are private or state-controlled multinationals in the same way as there are private or state-controlled uninationals.

Nevertheless, many uninational companies export a great deal; they remain uninational as long as they do not invest abroad in factories and/or offices, which would permit them to exercise their activities locally like an indigenous firm with legal status in the host country. A firm, for example, which exports its products by means of wholly independent import merchants is not a multinational. On the other hand, a firm which exports through its own subsidiaries *is* a multinational, if the subsidiaries have fixed assets like buildings, offices, warehouses or transportation equipment in the host country.

An example will clearly differentiate a uninational company from a multinational. A Scottish whisky distiller or French winemaker who exports to the United States through a New York import agent heads a uninational firm. If the same distiller or winemaker builds a distillery or buys vineyards and sets up business in California, Spain and Australia, he then manages a multinational.

This book has four main chapters. The first shows why and how the multinationals developed and in which countries and sectors they originated. The second chapter studies the internal functioning of the multinationals and their economic dimension. The third examines the role of the multinationals in the economy at national as well as international levels. Their role will be compared to that of uninationals in the areas of employment, inflation, recession, international trade, rates of exchange and the balance of payments. The final chapter analyses the involvement of the multinationals in the political, social and cultural domains.

On the basis of the information given in these four chapters, the conclusion tries to separate myth from reality in the images which we all have of the multinationals.

1   How Multinationals Developed

THE DIVERSITY OF THE HOME COUNTRIES

The multinational company is not the only form of international organization, nor is it the first that ever existed. From
earliest history – we have only to think of the Phoenicians
2500 years BC or the Venetians from the tenth century
through the Renaissance – merchants have traded on an
international basis. The same is true of bankers. Churches,
too, spread outside of their home territory, thanks to
missionaries.

The early modern multinationals were European. The first,
which dates from the beginning of the nineteenth century,
was the S. A. Cockerill steelworks, which was established in
Prussia in 1815 and today is Belgian-based. Others followed
at the end of the century – Bayer of Germany in 1863; Nestlé
of Switzerland in 1867; the Belgian Solvay in 1881; Michelin
(France) in 1893; and Lever Brothers (United Kingdom) in
1890. William Lever, founder of the last, explained that
'When customs duties and various restrictions hinder sales in
a country, it's time to build there.'[1]

THE FIRST MULTINATIONALS

At the turn of the century, transport costs and high duties
often made it difficult for industrialists to export. They
therefore decided instead to invest overseas. Some, like

7

Bayer of Germany went into Imperial Russia: others set up subsidiaries in Latin America. L'Air Liquide of France, with products difficult and expensive to transport, was one of the first to do this at the turn of the century. Its rival, the British Oxygen Company, now BOC, in contrast, went first into the markets in Australia and South Africa and other large Commonwealth countries where British influence was strong.[2] Other British companies like Lever Brothers, now the Anglo-Dutch giant, Unilever, also invested heavily in Africa. One interesting and unique early case was that of British American Tobacco (now B.A.T. Industries) which, from its formation in 1902, was always a multinational. It was banned from selling cigarettes in the British market, which was already overloaded with tobacco companies, so it was selling in Latin America, Africa and Asia right from its inception. Its subsequent development and growth in the United Kingdom has been in other industries like cosmetics, printing and packaging and retailing. It is now engaged on a second wave of multinationalization, moving into markets overseas in its new interests.

In the same way, as far as the primary sector of industry was concerned, the Europeans had to secure supplies of raw materials which did not exist in their countries – gold, copper, zinc, nickel, and petroleum, and bauxite later on. So they invested in the foreign countries where there were such resources and built the facilities necessary for their extraction.

The first phase of multinational growth was soon cut short. This happened in Russia following the 1917 Revolution, when all such enterprises were nationalized. Two successive World Wars created great problems for the parent companies. They were having enough difficulties in just surviving at home to try to develop their activities abroad. And, further, during the Second World War, the Government of the United States confiscated the German multinationals there. Their assets were sold to American firms. To give one example, Linde, the German gas company, had set up subsidiaries in the United States between the two Wars. These subsidiaries were confiscated and sold to Union Carbide, a large American chemical conglomerate. Union Carbide created a section for gas which was named the 'Linde Division'. Today, however, the German company has succeeded in reestablishing its own new subsidiaries in the United States.

THE AMERICAN PHASE

The best-known phase of multinational growth was basicaliy by American firms.[3] It began almost as soon as the Second World War ended in 1945 and continued to the end of the sixties, paralleling the reconstruction of Europe and the coming of the consumer society. For some years the United States, taking advantage of the wars between the European powers, had benefited from an impressive rate of growth. Above and beyond their own market, American companies were sending supplies to Europe, at a time when the growth of European firms was hampered by the successive wars. Thanks to superior technology, the Americans were exporting products which they were the first to manufacture. When the Europeans began to rebuild their economies, they obviously copied these products, either by developing their own technology or by importing American technology. The Americans had no choice but to go multinational. By this time they were suffering from local competition in Europe, because duties and transport costs had to be added to their production costs in the United States. To maintain their share of the market in Europe,[4] they had to build factories there. This phenomenon accelerated at the beginning of the sixties when the Common Market[5] gradually eliminated customs duties among the principal European countries. The Americans were thus able to consider the member countries of the EEC as a single market and set up factories to meet the scale of that market.

During the fifties and sixties, American companies intensified their efforts in setting up activities in Europe and Canada much more so than in Latin America, or other developing countries. This happened despite the fact that, in the latter countries, where the multinationals produce essentially for local consumption, labour is much cheaper and profitability much higher than in Europe. Thus it is clear that survival and growth are as important for the multinationals as profit.[6]

THE GROWTH OF EUROPEAN AND JAPANESE MULTINATIONALS

The development of European and Japanese multinationals began at the beginning of the seventies and produced a significant increase in the number of home countries of multinationals. The new multinationals were mainly Japanese and European, but they also originated in developing countries like Brazil, Mexico, India, Hong Kong, Singapore and South Korea, as well as in Eastern European countries. Today, therefore, the multinational phenomenon is becoming worldwide.

After the Second World War, the reconstruction of Europe and Japan led to the development of large uninational companies. These were very soon limited in their development because of the relatively small size of the economies of the countries in which they were based. Exporting within the Common Market, however, made rapid expansion possible for the European companies. Very often they could continue production in the factories in their home country and export to neighbouring countries thanks to the progressive lowering of customs and excise duties within the EEC. A network of subsidiaries dealing with distribution was quickly established in the countries to which they exported. This was not sufficient for some companies who found it necessary to set up factories in host countries.

There were four distinct reasons for this development:
1. In certain industries – for example, milk derivatives (with products which cannot be transported farther than 600 miles) or liquid gas (the containers are much too heavy) – there are production limits in any one factory. It is not advisable to

build huge factories, since the economies of scale in production are not enough to offset higher transport costs. It is far better to set up new factories in the countries where the customers are based. In contrast, in other industries like chemicals or steelmaking, it is possible to make such economies of scale that a large production unit in a single country is justified on grounds of profitability.

2. Local governments often prefer to have the multinationals invest in their countries rather than export to them. There are benefits in terms of local employment and an outflow of foreign currency can be avoided, resulting in a better trade balance for the host country.

3. Within the multinationals, local managements obviously prefer the parent company to set up a manufacturing plant in the host country because this makes the subsidiary more important within the group and at the same time facilitates relations with the host country.

4. Production in only one country leaves the company open to risks of war, nationalization or confiscation, or vulnerable to increases in duties or the establishment of import quotas or fluctuations in rates of exchange. Similarly, strikes in a single factory could halt sales to several countries at the same time.

After reconstructing themselves on a uninational basis and then at the European level (and so already becoming multinationals), these developing companies felt the need to go beyond Europe to secure further growth. In particular, they began to move into the United States and Canada. There it was possible to develop an immense new market, discover highly sophisticated products, advanced technologies and use a very important capital market. Moreover, the American capital market alone is greater than the international capital market (that of the various Euro-currencies: Euro-dollars, Euro-Deutsche-marks). In 1980, for example, the money supply was more than three times greater in the United States than the available funds on the international banking market at $1974 and $575 billion respectively.[7]

European companies have to a large extent met the 'American challenge', for the growth of European investment in the United States has been greater than that of American investment in Europe. In fact, from 1966 to 1980 the ratio of the stock of European investments in the United States to that of American investments in Europe has evened out – from 37 per cent to 49 per cent.[8]

The Japanese industrialists' international approach is totally different from that of the Europeans. In contrast to American or European industrialists, who conceive of products and services first of all in relation to their own country before thinking about exporting and setting up subsidiaries abroad, the Japanese have a global vision of the world. Living in a country with a very poor subsoil and having to import their raw materials, they have always had to export finished products to obtain the foreign currency necessary to pay for the import of raw materials. The Japanese have important trading companies spread throughout the entire world, known as the 'Sogo Shoshas' ('trading companies'). In many countries, these companies constitute networks of information on demand for new products. And the products manufactured in Japan are designed to satisfy the most common demands of the largest possible number of consumers around the world. As a result, Japanese factories produce in very large quantities from the moment they are set up. They benefit immediately from economies of scale and quickly accumulate experience in production techniques, which allows them to decrease unit costs. There are numerous examples of the successful application of this technique; the mass sales of electronic equipment, automobiles and even motorcycles – only a few years ago, who would have thought that the best motorcycles would not always be British?

Moreover, Japan has a further advantage in an excellent labour force. Workers are devoted to the heads of the company and rarely strike. When industrialization got underway in Japan, labour was very cheap compared to other developed countries. Even though this is no longer really the case, productivity, which is extremely high in international terms, means that the unit cost of labour compares favourably with Japan's competitors.

Lastly, the collaboration of government and industry in Japan is unique in the world. There is continuous collaboration between companies and the MITI (Ministry of Industry and International Trade). In fact, the greatest challenge at present is the Japanese challenge.

Within this third phase in the development of the multinationals, there is a rather limited move to establish factories in countries like Morocco, Tunisia or Vietnam. The output of these factories is destined not for local consumption but more for sale back in the industrialized countries. A typical example is Biderman, one of the big names in French ready-made wear. It built a plant in North Vietnam, because labour there is highly productive, cheaper than in other countries in South East Asia, and very reliable (so far there have been no strikes at all). For the same reasons, some firms create subsidiaries in Eastern European countries.[9] This form of multinationalization is generally limited to sectors like textiles, shoes, or mass consumption electronic equipment. It suits those industries in which labour represents a large part of production costs.

It is not always necessary for multinationals to involve themselves in direct foreign investment and set up their own factories to achieve the same result. Dunlop Holdings, the British-based rubber and sportsgoods manufacturers, is one of the world's biggest sellers of canvas shoes. Many of these come from a factory in South Korea, which is not owned by Dunlop. Under a factoring arrangement – in this case a transfer of technology – the shoes are made to exact Dunlop specifications, all production is overseen by Dunlop executives and the whole company takes the factory's entire output. The company gives reasons similar to those of Biderman for the decision to operate in this way – good labour relations, low costs and local skills.

Thus, at present, multinationals are generally American, European or Japanese. The multinationalization of firms is essentially a phenomenon of the industrialized countries: they are the homes of the multinationals and the countries in which the head offices are located. Moreover, the multinationals control and strengthen the setting up of their foreign subsidiaries in these same countries. Today new multinationals, originating in rapidly industrializing countries such as Brazil, Mexico, India and in South East Asia and Eastern Europe are being built up.

These elements have allowed multinationals of certain European countries and Japan to reinforce their position on the world market. Table 1.1 shows, for instance, that the book value of the foreign investments of Japanese companies which was a mere 0.1 per cent in 1914 rose to 2.7 per cent by 1971 following a set-back during and after the Second World War, and to 6.9 per cent by 1978. In Europe, the situation varies from country to country. The percentage of foreign investments declined for countries like Great Britain (from 45.5. per cent, to 14.8 per cent and to 11.9 per cent for the same years), Italy (from 8.7 per cent, 1.9 per cent and 0.9 per cent) or France (from 12.2 per cent, to 4.6 per cent to 3.9 per cent), increased for West Germany in the post-war period after a sharp fall, and for Switzerland and the Netherlands. American overseas direct investments rose 18.5 per cent in 1914 to 52 per cent in 1960, but declined thereafter to 43.5 per cent in 1978. The American multinationals have lost their preponderance in Latin America. For example, the share of the European multinationals in total direct investments in Brazil rose from 32 per cent in 1969 to 43 per cent in 1976, whereas the United States' share fell during the same period from 48 per cent to 32 per cent.[10]

Table 1.1 shows that 96.8 per cent of foreign investments in 1978 came from companies based in the eleven most highly developed countries in the world. The others represent only 3.2 per cent. None the less this percentage shows some increase, rising from nil in 1938 to 3.2 per cent forty years later.

Table 1.2 gives a precise idea of the recipient countries of the investments.

In 1978, almost 70 per cent of accumulated foreign direct investment was in developed countries with market economies and 28 per cent in developing countries. Compared with twenty years earlier, the development is clear; investments were being made less and less in developing countries in favour of the developed countries. Looking back 40 years, the contrast is even greater; 66 per cent of foreign investment in 1938 was going into developing countries.

There is therefore a dual shift, that is, a slight increase in the

TABLE 1.1   *Book Value of the Foreign Investments of the Principal Countries in the World (1914–78)*

Home country	Breakdown by percentage		
	1914	*1971*	*1978*
United Kingdom	45.5	14.8	11.9
West Germany	10.5	4.6	8.2
Switzerland	–	5.9	7.2
France	12.2	4.6	3.9
Netherlands	–	2.5	6.1
Sweden	–	1.5	1.6
Belgium-Luxemburg	–	1.5	1.2
Italy	8.7	1.9	0.9
Total Europe	76.9	37.3	41.0
United States	18.5	51.7	43.5
Japan	0.1	2.7	6.9
Canada	1.0	4.1	3.5
Total	96.5	95.8	94.9
Other countries (estimate)	3.5	4.2	5.1
General total	100.0	100.0	100.0
General Total in billions of dollars	14.3	160.2	386.2

SOURCE   Table based on John H. Dunning, *The History of Multinationals during the Course of a Century,* International Conference: Multinationals in transition, 15–16 November, 1982, University of Paris IX, Dauphine.

TABLE 1.2   *Host Countries for Foreign Investments*

Host country and group	1914	1971	1978
Total value of assets (in billions of dollars)	19.3	166.3	361.6
Breakdown of assets (by percentage)			
Developed countries with market economies:	37.2	65.2	69.6
Canada	5.7	16.8	11.9
United States	10.3	8.4	11.7
United Kingdom	1.4	8.1	9.0
Other Western European	6.4	20.4	28.7
Other European	9.9	neg.	neg.
Other countries	3.4	11.5	8.3
Developing countries:	62.8	30.9	27.8
Latin America	32.7	17.8	14.5
Middle East	2.8	2.1	2.3
Other countries	27.3	11.0	11.0
Total	100.0	100.0	100.0

SOURCE   John H. Dunning, op. cit.

number of home countries for multinational companies and a centering of their activities in the developed countries with market economies.

SECTOR DIVERSITY

There are three basic sectors of industry: raw materials, manufacturing, and services. In each case an example is given to illustrate the multinational phenomenon, as it is impossible to review nearly a century of history of all the sectors of the economy.

RAW MATERIALS: PETROLEUM

The petroleum industry really began in the United States in
the 1870s. After buying a refinery in Cleveland in 1865, John
Davidson Rockefeller set up the Standard Oil Company in
1870. At that time it already controlled ten per cent of the
American petroleum industry. In 1883, he incorporated the
Standard Oil Trust, a nationwide company. Two years later,
70 per cent of Standard Oil's output was being exported to
Europe and the Middle East.[11]

Rockefeller had succeeded in placing himself at the
strategic intersection between extraction and distribution:
that is, transportation. His fortune was based on the control of
the transport of sources of energy – control he already
possessed in the case of coal.

This control enabled Rockefeller to impose high charges to
both buyers and sellers of petroleum which did not come from
his wells and was not destined for his refineries. With the
fortune he rapidly accumulated over the years he bought up
almost the entire oil business in the United States. Such
practices violated the spirit of the anti-trust law (the Sherman
Act) voted in 1890 and, in May 1911, the Supreme Court
upheld a decision ordering Rockefeller to sell the 33 companies he then owned, apart from Standard Oil of New
Jersey.

This happened at a time when most petroleum, then called
illuminating oil, was used for lighting purposes. The two
largest petroleum producers in the world were the United
States (8.5 million tons in 1900) and Russia (10 million tons
for the same period). Later on, Russian output stagnated and
then decreased in the disorganization following on the
Revolution.[12] In Europe, except for Russia and, to a much
lesser degree, Germany, supply depended essentially on
American imports. As the years went on, however, new oil
fields were discovered in many parts of the world: Sumatra,
Borneo, Canada, Poland, Romania, Asia, and Peru (around
1905–10); later on Mexico (1920) and Venezuela (1930).
Europe was trying to be more and more independent and

European companies, as well as those in the United States, were obtaining important long-term concessions in oil-producing countries. These concessions were principally in the Middle East, beginning at the turn of the century.

Before the First World War, the world petroleum market was dominated by two large companies, Standard Oil of New Jersey and Royal Dutch/Shell, a joint Anglo/Dutch grouping, which had originally been two separate companies. Shell was set up by Marcus Samuel and named after his father's business, which had been importing shells for decorative purposes. Samuel had first found oil in Russia, but it was not long before he realized that, if he were to match the power of Rockefeller, he must compete in all markets. Rivalry between the two groups was intense. By 1893, Samuel had regular cargoes of oil going to the United States. Rockefeller offered to buy out Samuel, who refused and in 1897 Shell Transport and Trading was formed with Samuel holding one third of the stock and with his family in effective control.

Spurning other offers from the United States, Samuel preferred an agreement with Royal Dutch, a company run by Henri Deterding which had been competing with both Shell and Standard Oil. Samuel believed that his company was much stronger than Royal Dutch, but Deterding was younger and more ruthless than Samuel, who was now deflected from business by his civic and social life. When the oil trade slumped in 1903, Samuel was forced into a merger with Royal Dutch, not on equal terms as expected, but on forty-sixty to Deterding, with the latter as managing director. In 1906, Royal Dutch/Shell, perhaps the most international of companies, was formed.

All was not well for Shell in the United Kingdom either. Samuel had long agitated for the British Navy to turn from coal to oil for its ships. This led to some suspicion on the part of the Navy as the First World War loomed, as to the loyalties of Shell, opposition which was orchestrated by the then Mr Winston Churchill. When oil eventually began to be used by the Navy in 1910, the big contract went not to Shell but to Burmah Oil, a company formed after oil was found in Burma, then part of the British Empire. Around the same time, a new company had been set up to exploit the newly discovered oil reserves in the Middle East. Under pressure from Churchill, the Government decided in 1914 to buy a 51 per cent stake in this company, Anglo-Persian Oil. The price was £2 000 000. In Parliament, Churchill accused Shell and Standard Oil of monopolizing the world's oil trade and creating an artificially high price. Anglo-Persian Oil, which was eventually to become British Petroleum, had been formed in 1909, by Burmah Oil and William Knox D'Arcy, who had previously made a fortune in Australia's gold rush, retired to London where in 1901 he heard about a French geologist's report of immense reserves in Persia. D'Arcy negotiated an exclusive contract with Teheran for 480 000 square miles for £20 000 cash, a 16 per cent share in the profits and 20 000 shares of £1 each.

Naturally, the British Government protected its interest and, with its controlling interest, prevented any takeover bids from coming in. (It was not until the Conservative administration of Mrs Margaret Thatcher that the Government divested itself of control.) Unpopular among its rivals and suspected by many of the countries in which it set up business, British Petroleum flourished until 1951 when Dr Mossadeq, a new Iranian leader, nationalized BP's oilfields. BP was able, after initial difficulties, to organize a boycott. When Mossadeq fell from power two years later, however, BP had lost its monopoly in Iran, though it remained the biggest producer.[13]

In the early part of the century, therefore, the American and British groups virtually controlled the oil industry and, as the latter had no home resources, they have been multinational from their inception. European countries were content to remain dependent on these sources until the First World War. France, for example, was entirely dependent until 1914 on American, Russian or Romanian refineries for its oil supply. The difficulties of supply encountered at the end of the war led the French Government to establish conditions for the creation of a French petroleum industry: development of French crude oil resources, regulation of imports, a favourable position for French refining, development of a petroleum fleet flying the French flag, and creation of reserve stocks. All these measures brought about the birth of the Compagnie Française des Pétroles (CFP) in 1924, under the auspices of the Poincaré government. In 1928 an agreement was signed setting the terms for the association of the CFP and its partners: Anglo-Persian (which would become British Petroleum (BP) in 1954), Shell, and Near East Development (held equally by the companies known today as Exxon and Mobil). Each partner held 23.75 per cent. The remaining 5 per cent was allotted to Mr Gulbenkian, who had negotiated with the Arabs.

The Law of 25 July 1931 ratified the final status of CFP. The French Government's share is 35 per cent but it has 40 per cent of the votes at its disposal thanks to a system of shares with privileged voting rights.[14]

Until the end of the Second World War the price of petroleum remained very low, as demand was not especially great and oil was competing with coal all over the world. It became necessary to limit the oil supply to avoid a price collapse and therefore to limit the search for new oil deposits. Only towards the middle 1950s did oil become the world's number one source of energy, ahead of coal.

At that time, the oil world was really divided in two. There was the American market which was self-sufficient and the international market in which the Middle East was the main supplier for Europe. But working costs there were completely different. The petroleum extracted in the United States at that time cost ten times more than that extracted in the Middle East. The reason for this disparity was that in the United States the private individual actually owned the oil resources; in other countries, the government was the sole owner, granting concessions to companies exploiting the resource. The natural boundaries of an underground deposit of oil rarely correspond to the dividing lines of land ownership and at the time of the rush for 'black gold' this led to the proliferation of disorganized drilling in the United States which in turn brought a considerable increase in unit cost of crude extraction.

Confronted with this situation, several independent American companies like Conoco or Getty Oil decided in the 1950s to invest in the Middle East and extract petroleum there. Since oil was less expensive to extract, they reasoned that they could resell it in the United States and take away a share of the market from the 'Seven Sisters' in that way. But the Seven Sisters – the seven largest oil companies in the world – quite apart from the oil from their own deposits in the United States, were buying petroleum from small American companies extracting black gold from their fields in just the same way as farmers live off their land. There were numerous such small producers concentrated in the southern states of the USA and the petroleum imported from the Middle East brought the threat to them of being eliminated from the market. And the southern states are extremely important electorally for anyone who wishes to get to, or remain in, the White House. For this reason, President Eisenhower decided to set up import quotas for foreign petroleum in 1959. These quotas were based on the share of the market previously held by each company established in the United States. It was the heyday of the Seven Sisters, the most important of which is Exxon.[15] Of the six others, four are American: Standard Oil of California, Gulf Oil, Texaco and Mobil. One is British (British Petroleum) and the last is the Anglo-Dutch group, Royal Dutch/Shell.[16]

Once Eisenhower had set the quotas, the independent firms which had discovered oil in the Middle East found their American market closed. They no longer had any choice if they were to survive, but to turn to the international market which was supplying Europe and Japan.

But competition was great, all the more so in that new firms had been created in Italy (ENI), France (Elf-Erap), the Middle East, then in Venezuela, Indonesia, Algeria and Nigeria. Inflation was low at that time compared to the years to come and the price of a barrel of petroleum remained relatively stable in current prices between 1958 and 1972.

The purchasing power related to oil prices declined 16 per cent during the same period and this led the petroleum-exporting countries to join together to form OPEC: the Organization of Petroleum Exporting Countries. Gradually, all the large producers in the Third World became members of the organization, which put them in a better position to negotiate with the oil-consuming countries. First, there were renegotiations of the royalties paid by the oil companies and then the progressive recovery of the control of the sources of supply by the nationalization of the oil fields. Then came the unilateral setting of prices of crude oil, from September 1973. Moreover, the success of the price-fixing policy was helped because as the 1960s came to an end, the American market was no longer self-sufficient. This trend has continued and today the United States depends on oil imports for more than 50 per cent of its supply.

From 1973 to 1974, as a result of the oil shock, the price of a barrel of crude petroleum increased by 270 per cent. From 1974 to 1979, related purchasing power declined by only five per cent. This means[17] that over the past twenty years a barrel of petroleum has more than doubled its purchasing power.

Although there is no real petroleum multinational of Soviet origin,[18] the USSR is currently one of the largest producers of crude oil in the world. In 1978, out of a world total of 3067 million tons, the USSR produced 572.5 million tons, as opposed to 485 million tons for the United States.[19] This is enough at present for USSR domestic supply as well as that of the Comecon countries (the equivalent of the Common Market in Eastern European countries), but the oil fields in the Ural Mountains are becoming exhausted and no one knows whether the new sources discovered in Siberia and on the Chinese border will be sufficient to maintain the status quo. Any change from self-sufficiency to dependence on imports in Comecon could have serious consequences for the world market.

Thus, as the industry developed the oil companies themselves rapidly became multinational. The American companies first set up business in Europe, before Middle East oil began to be exploited, and later the European group established themselves principally in the Middle East.

At present, the petroleum multinationals can be divided into two large groups: the developed countries (the Seven Sisters and the American and European independent companies) and the OPEC countries. Their respective strengths are not the same. The former are stronger in distribution[20] and the latter in extraction. Only the future will reveal the evolution of the balance of power between the two groups.

Confronted with the current decline in the demand for oil and the strategic menaces of the new OPEC multinationals, the traditional multinationals have invested in the search for new sources of energy: coal distillation, solar energy, nuclear and wind power. But in their research, particularly in the nuclear field, they meet competition from firms in other industrial sectors (electricity, nuclear power) like Westinghouse or General Electric.

Moreover, nuclear research leads to what could be described as 'de-multinationalizing' in order to leave room for government-owned companies whose aim is to control such energy sources. Many governments no longer want to be at the mercy of private companies, which proved unable to cope with OPEC during 1973 and the following years when the oil price soared. They hope by controlling nuclear resources to avoid the severe shock which the developed economies suffered during those years.

*   *   *

Petroleum is a remarkable example of the historical evolution of the multinationals in the primary sector. The development of the strategic importance of raw materials led to the decision by many of the producing countries to control the resources of their own subsoil. The preferred form of such control is nationalization.

Moreover, the Seven Sisters – in part and unintentionally – are responsible for their loss of power. When the independent American companies decided to invest in the Middle East the

large companies countered by instigating the political decision to control imports made by President Eisenhower in
1959. This reaction to possible competition in this market had
incalculable repercussions that the Seven Sisters could doubt-
lessly not have foreseen. They lost control of the world
industry, a domination which had fed the mouth of their
all-powerfulness, and lost not to the benefit of the independent companies, but to that of OPEC. The result shed new
light on one of the myths attached to the large multinationals:
that of being able to foresee all.

The end of the reign of the Seven Sisters can be observed in
the figures. In 1963 they produced 82 per cent of the world's
crude oil. In 1975 their share fell to 30 per cent. At the same
time, governments which owned nine per cent of production
in 1963 controlled 62 per cent by 1975. The multinationals
were more successful in protecting their position in refining
and distribution since, during the same period, their share of
this market only declined by 18 per cent and 17 per cent[21]
that is, from 65 per cent to 47 per cent and from 62 per cent
to 45 per cent respectively.

An identical phenomenon took place in the copper mining
industry. Countries like Zaire, Zambia and Chile nationalized the multinational firms (mostly American or European)
which owned the mines. As a rule over the years the
multinationals have lost at least part of their control over the
sources of supply of raw materials, with the exception of
bauxite. Nevertheless, they have retained their full importance in these industries, thanks to their capabilities in
refining and distribution, and their technology.

Thus in 1948 the production of copper by the seven main
companies was 1 664 000 metric tons or 70 per cent of world
output. In 1978 this production, although it had gone up to
1 947 000 metric tons, only represented 25 per cent of world
output. The phenomenon can be explained by the discovery
of more and more abundant copper deposits throughout the
world, but also by the growing role of state-owned enterprises
in the exploitation of their own resources. Union Minière
(Belgian) was nationalized by Zaire in 1967. Chile and

Zambia nationalized American or British copper mining companies. The closer we get to the individual copper consumer, the more the multinationals have maintained their importance. Thus, in 1979 the American, Japanese and Canadian firms possessed 63 per cent of the smelting capabilities and 70 per cent of the refining capabilities of the five largest companies in the world.[22]

These examples all clearly illustrate the fact that the companies which invested mostly in the developed countries have suffered the least from nationalization. Thus, from 1960 to 1976 of the 1447 nationalizations which took place throughout the world, only 200 took place in developed countries.[23]

MANUFACTURING: AUTOMOBILES

The growth of multinational companies in automobile manufacturing was to begin with a European phenomenon, beginning at the end of the nineteenth century. In 1896 Daimler, the German-based company (later to become Daimler-Benz), set up a factory in England.[24] Then in 1899 it established an assembly plant in Vienna. The first production subsidiary, also in Vienna, was opened in 1902.[25] Already, in 1888, an American company had started working under a Daimler licence. The first American Mercedes were produced from this New York factory in 1904. Its activity ended with the First World War, in 1914. Fiat was another European automobile company which became multinational very early. It first opened a subsidiary in Vienna in 1907, another in Poughkeepsie (New York State) in 1909, and had a manufacturing plant in Russia as early as 1912.

The greatest phase of multinationalization in the automobile industry, however, came from the American groups, mainly Ford and General Motors. Ford was established in Canada as early as 1903. Later on its assembly facility was transformed into a manufacturing plant, because the duties imposed by the Canadian Government on imported parts became prohibitive. Later Ford set up shop in Europe, first in England (Manchester, 1911), followed by France (Bordeaux, 1913). The automobile world rapidly became mainly American. In 1914 American manufacturers were making 358 000 cars a year or 78 per cent of world production. A record was reached in 1929 when 84 per cent of world production, equal to 5 300 000 cars[26], was from companies whose parent companies were based in the USA.

How did this American domination come about? It happened mainly because the Europeans simply were not competitive. They were obsessed by the idea that the automobile was a preserve of the rich to replace their carriages and drivers. As a result, they manufactured only deluxe cars, which were very costly. The Americans, in contrast, aimed for a broader market with more popular cars, in particular Henry Ford's Model T. Higher output permitted mass production and consequently lower unit cost. American production increased so rapidly that the opening up of factories abroad became a necessity. At the same time, the European companies with their very limited production were merely exporting: they had no need or demand for foreign subsidiaries.

The world automobile market thus became rapidly Americanized and by 1920 Ford had assembly plants in twenty countries in the continents of Europe, Australia, South America, and in Japan, South Africa and India. In 1926, in order to avoid high transport costs, Ford set up its first local overseas manufacturing plant in England. In 1930, the first turnkey factory was built in the Soviet Union – one of the first-ever examples of the transfer of technology. General Motors and Chrysler followed in Ford's footsteps, but at the same time the Japanese decided to close their doors to foreign firms to encourage the development of their own automobile industry.

These developments meant that by the beginning of the Second World War the phenomenon of multinationalization had spread generally from the United States into Europe. The political realities of the war changed nothing: the large companies had to submit to them to preserve their share of the market. In 1933 for example, the German National Socialist Government increased customs duties so much that Ford was obliged to transform its assembly subsidiaries into manufacturing plants to maintain profitability. Then, as early as 1935, Ford was ordered to use 100 per cent German materials in all its models made in the Cologne factory. Later, in 1936 the German Government forced Ford to export from its German factory to earn foreign exchange. This meant that Ford had to reduce output in its factories in Britain, which until then had been the main suppliers for the European market. A further blow was the freezing of the profits of Ford's German company and the Government's order that it should develop production of heavy-duty conveyances to be used for military purposes.[27]

In 1939, just before the outbreak of the war, only two large multinational automobile companies existed – Ford and General Motors. Of Ford's total output 23.2 per cent was produced abroad, broken down to 35.7 per cent in Canada, 40.5 per cent in the United Kingdom, 19 per cent in Germany and 0.42 per cent in France. The figures for General Motors were 19.6 per cent produced overseas (21.9 per cent in Canada, 23.4 per cent in the United Kingdom, and 54.7 per cent in Germany).[28]

During the war, the subsidiaries of the multinationals located in countries at war faced severe difficulties. In general, the managers of subsidiaries collaborated with the governments of the host countries in which they were based. This was true even when they were in countries at war with the countries in which the head office was located. So it was that the British subsidiary of Ford Motor of America contributed to the Allied effort and its German subsidiary to that of the Axis powers.

This attitude, however, did not always ensure safety and survival. Several years before, during the Spanish Civil War, the manager of the General Motors' subsidiary had been working peaceably with the Republican Government. The day in 1936 when Franco came to power everything changed. The immediate reaction was brutal: the manager found himself in jail. Because of this, relations between the multinational in question and Franco's Government were impaired for a long time.

After the Second World War, the automobile industry had an exceptional rate of growth. In 1979, the United States companies were producing well above their 1929 record: 8 434 000 cars compared with 5 300 000. It was during the post-war period that Europe, too, began mass production and exporting. The creation of the Common Market and the consequent lowering of customs duties among member countries, however, allowed American companies to consider Europe as a single market. In their local factories, the Americans manufactured models which were different from those they sold in the United States. They built small and medium-sized cars and began to compete with their European counterparts on their own ground. But the growth of US firms was slower than that of European companies: in 1938, the American share was 320 584 units, or 29.3 per cent of European production; by 1973, the figure was 3 139 995, or 24.1 per cent of European production.[29]

Production increased considerably in Latin America as well, although these countries followed a policy which was totally different from that of Europe. Until the end of the 1950s, the automobile multinationals (most of them American) sent parts manufactured in the United States to the three largest Latin American markets of Mexico, Argentina and Brazil where they were locally assembled. This was a rational policy, because import duties on components were generally very low, but were extremely high on finished products. Later, however, to counter the deficit in their balance of payments, the three countries raised their customs duties substantially on all imported products, except the machines necessary for manufacturing the parts used in assembling cars. Moreover, each car made locally had to have up to 99 per cent locally-produced components. Nevertheless, the American firms accepted these Draconian conditions for two reasons – they could keep their share of the market and the governments allowed them to repatriate all their profits.

The automobile production of these three countries was taking place almost entirely within their own territories, even though it was due to the activity of subsidiaries of foreign multinationals. To facilitate exports, as early as the beginning of the 1970s, the three countries lowered the required quotas of locally-made components to approximately 80 per cent for Brazil and Argentina and 60 per cent for Mexico. The quotas were further lowered to 40 per cent, if exports compensated for the imports. This was certainly an efficient policy for these Latin American countries, all the more so in that their own markets were growing rapidly. They also attracted investment from European firms such as Volkswagen, Fiat and Renault.[30] This led to a decline in the relative share of American investments in Latin America in favour of the European firms.

Before 1973, each continent was more or less autonomous as far as its automobile production was concerned. Of course multinationals existed, but they were producing mainly where they were selling. Only European and Japanese firms were exporting, principally to the United States. After 1973, the situation changed when the price of oil almost trebled. In order to maintain independence in energy and political strategy, and correct the balance of payments, the Nixon administration set up strict norms for petrol consumption, which had never before been limited. In 1980 all cars made in the United States had to get at least 20 miles to a gallon of petrol. The goal for 1985 was around 28 miles per gallon. American companies were therefore obliged to build smaller, lighter cars – the same type of cars that the Europeans and the Japanese had been making for years. This led to progressive standardization of car models with important repercussions on the worldwide organization of production. For economic reasons, a certain component (for example, gearboxes) could now be manufactured in only one country rather than in several, and supply the whole world market. In a way, this spelled the end of the self-sufficiency of the various continents at least as far as the components of an automobile were concerned.

The automobile sector is now producing a relatively mature product which no longer changes much, except for a few technological innovations. This mass product varies mainly by only marketing and advertizing. Nevertheless, there is still a huge market, shared primarily by Europe (13 420 000 cars in 1979), the United States and Canada (9 322 000) and Japan (6 176 000).[31]

The history of the internationalization of the automobile industry shows clearly that some of the changes in strategy were not made by the multinationals alone. In their relations with governments they are extremely influential and certainly had a great deal of weight in the reinforcement of the protectionist reactions of their respective countries. But their decisions concerning the choice of where or which models to produce are made partially in accordance with the governments' regulations. Germany and Italy before and during the Second World War and later on the Latin American countries are good examples. These governments, by administrative means (customs duties or quotas of locally-made components), were able to force the multinationals to manufacture rather than simply assemble in their countries. And today the Government of the United States is perhaps about to succeed in doing what European and Japanese competition have not been able to do, that is, make the giants of Detroit reduce the size of their normally huge cars by limiting the use of petrol.

SERVICES: THE BANKS

It is probably unfair to say that the first multinational banks were European banks, because during the nineteenth century the British and French set up subsidiary banks in their colonies. These host countries were, however, not independent – they were French or British territory, spoke the same language and used the same currency. The banks established

there can only be described as multinationals if an independent legal status is given to these host countries a posteriori; it
was not the case at the time. Nevertheless, through their
activities, the English and French banks acquired experience
in banking in faraway countries with economic, political and
social characteristics very different from those of the home
country.

The first truly post-imperial multinational banks were
American. In 1913, four of them had six subsidiaries abroad.
Seven years later, in 1920, the American banks were working
with about one hundred subsidiaries overseas, a figure which
varied little until 1950. The spectacular expansion of the
banking multinationals dates from the 1960s. The American
banks, which had 124 subsidiaries abroad in 1960, had 532
ten years later. In 1978 there were 761. There are two
explanations for this: first of all, these American banks were
following the growth of the investments of their business
clients in Europe, and banks must offer their clients, even
abroad, the services they are used to having at home. If not,
other banks will take over. Then, there is a reason particular
to the United States, where banks are not permitted to set up
business elsewhere in the USA, other than in the state where
they originate. Unable to work on a nationwide basis, they
very quickly became multinationals. This explains, for
instance, why the Bank of America can work only in
California within the United States, or Citicorp only in the
State of New York, but they can have as many subsidiaries as
they wish in any country of their choice, so long of course, as
foreign banks are permitted to operate in the host country.
Moreover, any foreign bank can set up subsidiaries anywhere
in the United States.

Of the 300 most important banks in the world 84 are
multinationals, of which 64 are among the first 100 and 43 in
the first 50.[32] Without exception, all these banks originate in
developed countries. In 1981, however, the largest bank in
the world was the French Crédit Agricole, which is not listed
as a multinational. One reason for this is that France's
banking sector is highly concentrated: the number of French

banks is relatively low compared to most of the other industrialized countries. What is more, the largest are state-owned. Thus, of the ten largest banks in the world four are French, of which three are highly multinationalized (and nationalized 100 per cent): the BNP, the Crédit Lyonnais and the Société Générale.

Of the 84 multinational banks, only three are Swiss and they are classified 27th, 32nd, and 48th respectively. Thus, contrary to the widespread stereotype of the 'gnomes of Zurich', the Swiss banks are not the most powerful in international terms. They come far behind the American, Japanese, French, British and German banks in amount of gross deposits and loans.[33] They do play an important role, but it is mainly in the interbank market (loans between banks).

Since 1965, the American banks have lost their relative importance. Of the top 50 banks in the world, their share of the deposits went from 42 per cent to 15 per cent in 1978. The same is true for the British and Canadian banks, which, over the same period, declined in this domain from 13 per cent to 7 per cent and from 9 per cent to 3 per cent respectively. In the case of Britain, all the clearing banks and merchant banks (members of the Accepting Houses Committee) are highly multinationalized as a result of the country's imperial past. Interestingly, though the British banks were among the first to move overseas, they have never been particularly prominent among the biggest banks. In 1965, only 4 of the top 20 were British and by 1980 this had dropped to 3. In contrast, the Japanese banks increased their share of deposits from 16 per cent to 29 per cent, the French banks from 5 per cent to 14 per cent and the German banks from 6 per cent to 17 per cent.[34] This evolution parallels the relative evolution of the companies of these countries albeit more extensively. We saw in Table 1.1 earlier that, between 1971 and 1978 the book value of foreign investments of the United States dropped from 51.7 per cent to 43.5 per cent of the total, from 14.8 per cent to 11.9 per cent for the United Kingdom and that, on the contrary, it increased from 2.7 per cent to 6.9 per

cent for Japan and from 4.6 per cent to 8.2 per cent for West
Germany. France is an exception to the general trend. In fact,
although the French companies have lost some of their
relative importance in international investment (from 4.6 per
cent to 3.9 per cent), the large French banks have reinforced
their world position. This is explained above all by the
concentration of the French banking sector which benefited
fully from the very rapid economic growth of France after the
Second World War, but partly also because the large French
nationalized banks have pursued intensely aggressive policies
overseas.

Two-thirds of the activities of the multinational banks –
which as mentioned earlier all originate in developed countries – are concentrated in their own countries. The remaining
third is divided into two parts: 60 per cent of which is in
developed countries and the rest in developing countries.[35]
These banks have highly compartmentalized activities, principally of five different kinds:
1. *Deposit banks* dealing with individuals or small businesses.
   Their activities consist essentially of small loans and
   deposits.
2. *Trade banks* working on a large scale, in particular with the
   large uni- or multinational companies, and with governments (mainly those of the developing countries) to
   finance the deficit in their balance of payments.
3. The banks which are part of the *money market* serving as
   intermediaries for other banks.
4. Banks primarily financing *foreign trade*.
5. Banks specializing in *portfolio management* managing
   private and corporate fortunes.
Banking activities are usually subject to strict national
regulations which limit their fields of activity. These regulations naturally vary from country to country. A few countries,
however, like the United Kingdom and Germany, authorize
so-called 'universal' banks which may carry on business in all
the five areas defined above at the same time. The same is
true for the Netherlands and, to a lesser extent, Switzerland.
On the other hand, the United States and Japan do not allow

their deposit banks to issue stock. In France and Italy, the deposit banks are constrained by government intervention in the loans they are allowed to make. The regulations vary as the governments use the regulation of credit as part of their policies to control inflation, rather than leaving it to market forces, as is the case in the United Kingdom.

As for their activities abroad, the banks again differ according to their home country as well. Thus American, British, Canadian and French banks have both commercial and deposit activities, which German, Japanese or Swiss banks do not. Moreover, the American and Swiss banks prefer to deal in industrial financing, whereas German and Japanese banks undertake direct loans or refinancings which are riskier.

*   *   *

This brief analysis of nearly a century of history of the multinationals shows that we are not talking about the evolution of a continuous phenomenon where growth is natural and inevitable. Their development, however, was by no means uniform – the two World Wars and the oil shock of 1973 were important breaks.[36] The phenomenon first spread between Europe and the United States; today the multinational firms are beginning to multiply in rapidly industrializing countries such as Brazil, Mexico, Argentina or India and, to a lesser extent, the Eastern European countries. Not all multinationals are gigantic enterprises – they can be small or medium-sized. Similarly, they are not all private: there are also state-controlled multinationals. The multinationals began in all the different sectors, but the most important originated in raw materials and manufacturing industries. Today, however, they are moving into new sectors, in particular the service industries. This movement is, however, relatively limited, for many services are by nature either public or limited to a single country such as: education, health, transport, security (army and police) and administration.

Their development shows, too, that despite their definite

economic weight, multinational companies are not totally masters of their own destiny. Governments can play an important role, particularly when they wish to promote local industry. They usually follow two courses of action: they may establish excessively high customs barriers and at the same time require certain quotas of locally-made components in all finished goods, as happened in the automobile industry before the war in Germany and Italy, or in the 1960s in Latin America. Alternatively, they may use nationalization, as was the case for raw materials such as petroleum or copper, which explains why multinationals have become much less important in the extraction of raw materials.

Thus the historical answer to the question of the relationships between multinationals and governments is that the former can only yield and adapt to the national sovereignty of the latter.

2 How Multinationals Function

INTERNAL ORGANIZATION

How do the multinationals function, first of all internally and, then, what is their economic importance in the countries in which they operate?

The multinational phenomenon is not new as the previous chapter shows, because certain companies have been in existence for more than a century. Many of these were able to survive wars, economic crises and technological changes. Others were nationalized, partially or totally, or absorbed by more successful firms. In fact, their behaviour has been guided by a number of principles or objectives, which were apparent throughout their history – survival, profit and growth. The objectives can be achieved during a period which may be of any length, but long-term success is never guaranteed.

OBJECTIVES

Survival: an enterprise is a living organism whose sole aim is not merely to earn money for the entrepreneur and his stockholders. It must provide a living for suppliers and employees and workers and furnish goods and services for clients who need them for their own survival. It also contributes to the profits of banks and financial institutions, from which it borrows and then repays at interest, and to the activities of governments to which it pays taxes.

Profit: any business organization must be profitable, or it will have greater difficulty than its competitors in raising capital from financial institutions or shareholders for the research and development in new factories, or to pay suppliers and employees enough to ensure the highest level of participation on their part.

Growth: if the company does not grow at least at the same pace as the national and foreign competition it faces, it will lose its share of the market. If it fails to do this, profits cease and ultimately the very survival of the whole enterprise is threatened.

State-owned multinationals often have the same objectives as privately-owned companies, as they are usually managed in the same way. Should they show a temporary deficit, subsidies are allotted from the government budget to compensate for any constraints for profitability which arise from the necessity to provide a public service. But such situations cannot go on indefinitely, even though growth is not necessarily one of their objectives. The only objective of a state-owned enterprise – above and beyond its public service mission – therefore becomes survival.

In the multinationals the objectives of survival, profit and growth can be defined at two levels: that of the group and that of the subsidiaries. They may be modified depending on the country in which the subsidiary is located. For example, the management can take an altogether more short-term view for a subsidiary located in a country where the political risks are larger (war, revolution, riots, nationalization . . .) than for the group as a whole. For a developing country, growth objectives can be a function of the state of development of the market: they can be more important than those of the parent company, or the total group. Profit objectives are not uniform either. In certain countries with high rates of inflation and interest such as Brazil or Israel, a much greater profitability in local currency will be required of the subsidiary than of the home-based parent company. Even in local currency, the desirable level of profits will be larger if the country is considered a high risk investment. In contrast, lower profits will be required on a short-term basis, if the long-term growth of the market is very promising.

It is clear then that a multinational company's objectives vary from subsidiary to subsidiary, but in every case they are essentially economic. It follows that they have important social and cultural consequences on the creation of wealth, employment and patterns of consumption. But in each of these areas the multinational company is in contact with other social actors such as governments, labour unions, or different associations which can counter, control, or reorganize the social consequences. The success of the multinational depends therefore as much on the reactions of the other forces in society which interact with and influence it, as it does on the company's competitors.

ORGANIZATION, BUDGET AND PLANNING

All multinationals, whether small or medium-sized companies, large enterprises, giants, or very well-known businesses,[1] confront complex organizational systems wherever they are set up. In fact, they must deal with a different situation in each country in which they are established. Each host country is led by a government which both embodies and interprets national sovereignty. The rules of one administration are unlikely to mirror those of another country, even a neighbouring one. The same is true in economic, social and monetary situations. And one should not forget the differences due to the varying cultures, which follow upon the history of each nation. This means that the management of the foreign subsidiaries can be a delicate problem. The products manufactured and sold by the local subsidiaries have to be adapted to the specifications of the host country (for example, Ford automobiles manufactured in Europe for the European market) or on the contrary be the same as those of the parent company and the other subsidiaries, called sister subsidiaries (for example, refrigerators and washing machines). The selection and training of indigenous workers and staff must take into account the availability of labour and local customs and habits which cannot be entirely modified by the multinational company's subsidiary.

Taken by itself, the subsidiary of the multinational company functions in a way similar to a uninational company in the host country. But taken as a group, the multinational is something more than simply the total of its different subsidiaries. It benefits from the experience of each subsidiary and can transmit the various skills learned to its member companies. These may include technology and financial capabilities, marketing, human resources (managers can move from one subsidiary to the next), and research done by the parent company or the sister firms.

In general, multinational companies are organized in three different ways:

1. Companies which have highly diversified activities (for example, B.A.T. Industries, which manufactures tobacco, cosmetics and has printing and packaging and retailing interests, or Rank or Hovis McDougall) have a vertical organization compartmentalized by product on a world-wide basis.

2. Horizontally, by geographical area. Ultramar, the oil company is one British example. Each area has its management (for example, Europe or the Far East), which coordinates the activities of the subsidiaries located there. This type of organization is far less common in the United Kingdom than vertical integration. The reverse is true in France.

3. The huge multinationals like Unilever or Philips have a matrix form of organization which combines regional and product group organization.

The most important development in the relations between the parent company and its subsidiary is that of the establishment of the budget. To begin with, the general management of the foreign subsidiary drafts a budget based on its forecast of sales, expenses and profit margin. Next, the proposed budget is studied by the general management of the parent group in relation to the objectives of the subsidiary. Only then, when the budgets of all the subsidiaries have been approved, does the general management of the parent company decide its total budget at the international level. From then on, the subsidiaries send regular activity reports to the parent company, from which it can study and require explanations of any eventual deviations from the initial budget.

In many cases, there is a three- or five-year plan for the main foreign subsidiaries. Such a plan is then incorporated in the overall planning of the total group. Certain multinationals, however, only plan at group level. Such a plan is only a means of trying to forecast future trends; the actual decisions made within the company do not implement the plan. Moreover, very often the executives who participate in the elaboration of the corporate plan do not take part in strategic decision-making. In the same way, the decision makers feel very free to ignore the plan when making local decisions.

DECISION-MAKING

Who then makes the decisions within the multinationals, and how are they made? Is the process any different from that of the uninational firms? The answer seems to come too quickly, as in an easy classroom exercise: the process must be much more complicated in the multinationals – the men must be more intelligent and have access to sophisticated computer information in making decisions. It is also relatively easy to imagine an all-powerful chairman hidden in his office making all the decisions. In fact in the multinationals, the way in which a decision is made depends on the type of decision which is to be made. There is, therefore, a hierarchy of decisions, which can be readily distinguished as follows:
1. *Strategic decisions*, which determine the general orientations of the organization. The general management of the group determines these directions. In the multinationals,

they are the result of a long political process, following detailed negotiations between the headquarters of the parent company and its subsidiaries.[2]

2. *Administrative decisions* establish the situational context of the managers of an organization: the organization chart, job descriptions, the system of reward and punishment. Once again, these decisions are the result of a process of discussion between the general management of the group and the managements of its foreign subsidiaries. Budget decisions come into this category.

3. *Policy decisions* create a predetermined answer for repetitive acts. Policy decisions are made within the general context of strategic decisions but at lower levels, for example, at the level of administrative or financial management, marketing or production. There is always some contact between the corresponding management levels of the parent company and the subsidiary.

4. *Operational decisions* are those decisions which cannot be foreseen within the framework of strategic, administrative or policy decisions. They leave a margin for initiative for those who make them. Such decisions have to do with what is called the management of the foreign subsidiaries. The general management does not intervene, either in a multinational or uninational group with production and distribution subsidiaries abroad or within the home country.

A great deal of power within a multinational group can be at stake for those involved in certain decisions. If a group does not have the means to invest simultaneously on two continents, Africa and America, for example, it will have to choose between the two. This choice will depend on whether the regional manager for Africa or the regional manager for America has more influence with the chairman and the board of directors. Each will promote his region and also his own present and future position within the group.

In this hierarchy of decisions it is clear that, whatever the decision to be made in a multinational or uninational organization, the final result will always follow an internal work process centred on the relations between the actors. This goes against the tenacious stereotype of the all-powerful chairman making important decisions all alone thousands of miles away. Moreover, the previous chapter has shown that the results of the decision do not depend solely on the multinational itself which is making the decision: competitors, governments, labour unions and consumers all play a part.

It is also true that the confidence of the chairman of the group in the managers of the foreign subsidiaries is a much more important element in decision-making than the results of the most sophisticated and beautifully presented studies which are also part of the process. In fact, local managers implement the decisions in their own subsidiaries. The results depend a great deal more on the managerial qualities of the person in question than on the value of the studies which preceded the decision. These privileged relations between the chairman and the managers personalize the processes which link the parent company to its subsidiaries. Moreover, the people involved know each other well and work on a basis of reciprocal confidence.

ECONOMIC IMPORTANCE

We will now deal successively with the size and the growth of the multinationals.

SIZE

This section will look at the size of the multinationals compared with that of the host countries where they carry on their activities, and then analyse the importance of the multinationals in the total industrial activity of the host countries. Lastly, the overall size of the multinationals compared with their home countries' operations will be reviewed.

The multinationals and the host countries

The economic importance of the multinationals can be measured by different variables: the turnover (sales), the value added, total profit, the number of employees, capital stock or annual investments. Whatever system is chosen it must be such that the same variable can be used to compare multinationals with other organizations. However, the comparisons made with regard to multinationals are not always proper. It is possible nevertheless to list their turnover, their number of employees and those of other, uninational economic organizations such as the postal services or the railroads. The parallels between the number of employees in the multinationals and those in government agencies (of which the army is almost always the largest) must be handled with care, since the latter are not all economic entities.

What is the significance of a comparison of the economic importance of the multinationals and that of the countries where they carry on their activities? If we want to measure their respective powers, economic importance on its own is not enough. Clearly, countries are not organizations. The United Kingdom, for example, is a political, social and cultural entity as well as an economic one. It is a geographical area made up of organizations, political parties and associations, government agencies and private and state-owned companies. But the United Kingdom is above all a society with a history and political and legal institutions which produce the decisions considered legitimate by its citizens. The decisions become necessarily a part of civic life (for example, the right to abortion in certain conditions) and economic life (the nationalizations of the Labour administrations after 1945 and the current 'privatizations' of the Conservative administration). The first section of Chapter 3 will show that, in case of conflict, governments of whatever size have sufficiently powerful means to impose their point of view on companies whether they are multinational or not.

In seeking simply to make an economic parallel between multinationals and countries two caveats must be observed.

The first is to clarify the geographical scope of both. The production of wealth by multinationals takes place within numerous national territories; the production of a country, in contrast, within a single nation. But, since most of the very largest multinationals originate in the most highly industrialized countries (the USA, Great Britain, Germany, Japan) and they carry out more than half of their activities in those same countries it is easy to assume that their size is often comparable to that of the total economies of small countries. For example, in 1981 the number one company in the world according to turnover was Exxon with $113 billion (worldwide sales). If we were to compare this figure with that of the GNP of the different nations using the same year, Exxon would be seventeenth after Iran (GNP: $120 billion) and before Sweden (GNP: $112 billion). As for the United Kingdom, it comes sixth with $504 billion, behind (in order): the United States ($2937 billion), the USSR: ($1348 billion), Japan ($1127 billion), West Germany ($682 billion) and France ($568 billion).[3] As the GNP of the USA is twenty-four times greater than that of Iran, it can seem possible at first glance that Exxon – the largest American enterprise according to turnover – is of a worldwide economic size equivalent to Mexico.

But this is not the case. Actually, a second precaution which must be taken when trying to make an economic comparison between multinationals and countries is to do it with the same means of measurement. And the GDP of a country and the turnover of a firm are not comparable. (Gross Domestic Product (GDP) is always very close (+/− 1%) to Gross National Product (GNP). Exports must be added to the former and imports subtracted in order to obtain the latter.)

The first is what is called an economic aggregate. It gives the dimension of the economy of the country studied. If we try to calculate the size of a company in comparison with that of the economy of a country we must know the 'value added' produced by each. That produced by the firm is made up of salaries, annual depreciation, changes in inventories, taxes paid to the government and dividends paid to shareholders.

TABLE 2.1 *Value Added of the Local Subsidiaries of Multinational Firms in Percentages of the GDP of Some Developed Countries*[a]

Country	Percentage of manufacturing production due to the firms with foreign capital[b]	Value added of the manufacturing industry in percentages of the GDP in 1976[c]	Correcting factor[d]	Value added due to the foreign multinationals in percentages of the GDP[a]
United States	3[e] (1974)	24		2.2 (1974)
Japan	5.1 (1975)	35[f]	1.65 (1971)	2.9 (1971)
Germany	25.1 (1972)	37	1.54 (1973)	14.3 (1973)
United Kingdom	14.7 (1973)	25	1.40 (1974)	5.1 (1974)
France	24.5 (1975)	27	1.47[g]	9.71
Canada	51 (1974)	19	2.45 (1974)	23.7 (1974)

NOTES

a. For some countries, the following data are available: the percentage of the value added in manufacturing due to the firms with foreign capital (column b), the percentage of the value added of the manufacturing industry in relation to the gross domestic product (sum of the value added of all the sectors) (column c), and the ratio of total foreign investment in the country to foreign investment in the manufacturing industry in the same country, called the 'correcting factor' in column d. The value added due to the foreign multinationals in each of these countries is then obtained by multiplying one by one the figures of column b by those of column c and then multiplying that result by the correcting factor in column d. The use of the correcting factor implies an assumption that the value added in manufacturing is analogous with that of the other sectors. The results of this table over-estimate the size of the multinationals in comparison with the economies of the host countries since column b includes as a 'multinational' any company in which foreign capital is larger than 20 per cent.

b. *Penetration of Multinational Enterprises in Manufacturing Industry in Member Countries: Statistics Updated at the End of 1978* (OECD, 1979), p. 73. For France, Canada and the United Kingdom: value added. For Japan and West Germany: production.

c. *Handbook of International Trade and Development Statistics*, UNCTAD (United Nations 1979), pp. 506–7.

d. *Penetration of Multinational Enterprises in Manufacturing Industry in Member Countries* (OECD, 1977), pp. 29–31.
   For example: for Germany: 100/64.9 = 1.54

e. The United States is the only country for which the figures are directly available: Ned G. Howenstine, 'Gross Product of US Affiliates of Foreign Companies', *Survey of Current Business* (1979), Table 4, p. 30.

f. 1974 figure for Japan.

g. For France, estimate made by averaging the figure for Germany and the figure for Great Britain.

That of the country is obtained by adding up all the wealth –
the 'value added'[4] – produced annually by all its economic
agents including companies. As for turnover, it is a micro-
economic variable. It is, in fact, made up of the value added
and the intermediate consumption of goods and/or services
coming from other companies, purchases of energy, raw
materials and components which are essential to production.
The value added at the level of a company is therefore less
than turnover: in general, one-third. So, if the turnover of a
company and that of its supplier are added together, the value
added of the latter is included twice and the value added of *its*
suppliers several times. This is what is done systematically by
all those who compare the GNP of a country with the
turnover of a company. To return to the example of the world
position of Exxon and the economic importance of Mexico,
the economic agents of the latter – including the local
subsidiaries of the multinationals – produce within its border
a value added (which is a contribution to the GDP) probably
more than three times larger than that of Exxon at the
worldwide level.

The only precise way to estimate the weight of an economic
agent within the economy of a country is to know the total
value added of this agent. The same is true for the importance
of the foreign multinationals in a country: we must know the
value added ascribed to the local subsidiaries of these
multinational firms of foreign origin. Not surprisingly, few
statistics exist in this area, but estimates are possible and
Table 2.1 gives the results.

Table 2.1 illustrates important differences between the
United States, Japan, the three main European countries and
Canada. The United States has been little penetrated by
foreign investment. This can be explained by the technological advance of its companies and the high cost of local labour.
Its European and Japanese competitors preferred to export
to the US from factories located in their countries, rather than
trying to build or acquire factories in the United States.
Nevertheless, it seems possible that the percentage of foreign
investments in the total economy of the United States has

increased since 1974 (the date of the figures in Table 2.1). Several factors explain this evolution: firstly, the increase in the cost of labour in Europe and Japan; secondly, the decline of the dollar until 1980, especially in relation to the German Deutsche Mark, the Swiss Franc and the Dutch Guilder; and lastly, the relative decline of the American technological advantage over other countries.

Japan is a country which has been traditionally closed to foreign investment since it refused for a long time, and still avoids majority foreign holdings in its firms, even though recently it has relaxed its rules in this area. It is natural that Japan has been and is likely to remain very little penetrated by foreign firms.

Of the main three European economies, manufacturing industry in France and Germany is heavily penetrated by foreign firms (24.5 per cent and 25.1 per cent respectively). The German manufacturing sector is proportionally larger than the French manufacturing sector in relation to the total economy (37 per cent as against 27 per cent) and services in general are much less penetrated by foreign investment than is industry. Thus it is natural that the weight of the foreign firms in Germany's economic activity is larger than in France (14.3 per cent as against 9.7 per cent respectively). In 1973, foreign investment in the United Kingdom was equal to 14.7 per cent of manufacturing output, a low proportion at least as compared with France and Germany. As 25 per cent of the value added of the British economy is due to its manufacturing sector, the weight of the foreign firms in its gross domestic product is much lower at 5.1 per cent than that of the two other European countries for which figures are available. Nevertheless, since Great Britain joined the Common Market in 1973 there has been very heavy local investment on the part of American multinational firms. In fact, they have a tendency to use the UK rather than the other member countries of the EEC, possibly because of the common language, as a bridgehead for Europe. It is therefore possible that in recent years the relative importance of the foreign multinationals in the British economy has increased.

TABLE 2.2　Share in Manufacturing Industry of Firms with Foreign Capital (percentage of production)

International classification by industry	United States[a]	Japan	Germany	United Kingdom[b]	France	Canada
Manufacturing industry (total)	3	5.1	25.1	18.7	27.8	56.2
Food, drink, and tobacco	7	1.4	19.3	14.3	—	38.3
Textiles, clothing, and leather industry	3	0.3	—	5.3	8.6	33.7
Timber and wood products including furniture	1.3	0.0	—	1.2	10.6	18.9
Paper and paper products, printing, and publishing	5	1.0	—	10.6	13.5	33.9
Chemical industry and chemical products, petroleum derivatives, coal derivatives, rubber and plastic products	14	6.3	43.5	38.2	45.1	90.2

Non-metallic mineral products excluding petroleum and coal derivatives	4	5.9	—	8.0	17.6	52.5
Basic metallurgy	—	0.1	36.7	9.0	18.1	17.4
Metal products, machinery, and equipment	9.3	0.5	25.3	21.1	25.3	71.5
Other manufacturing industries	5	7.8	—	21.6	15.4	48.8

SOURCE   Penetration of multinational enterprises in manufacturing industry in member countries: statistics updated at the end of 1978. OECD, 1979, Table 2a, p. 4.

NOTES

a. Figures from Table 4, p. 30, in Ned G. Howenstine, 'Gross Product of US Affiliates of Foreign Companies', *Survey of Current Business* (January 1979).

b. Figures of the share of companies with foreign capital in the manufacturing sector in the United Kingdom from Table 2b, p. 6. Foreign capital between 20 per cent and 50 per cent.

Canada has traditionally had an economy heavily penetrated by foreign capital (51 per cent), particularly American
capital. At 19 per cent its manufacturing sector is a relatively
small part of its total economy, making the total share of GDP
due to foreign multinational firms 23.7 per cent.

The penetration of multinationals in the manufacturing
industries varies according to sectors. Table 2.2. gives some
idea of this. Certain industries are heavily multinationalized
in terms of output (the chemical industry is one example) and
the variations according to countries are considerable: 90.2
per cent for Canada, 38.2 per cent for the United Kingdom,
but only 6.3 per cent for Japan. Other industries like textiles
and clothing are much less multinationalized: 6.2 per cent for
the United Kingdom and 0.2 per cent for Japan.

Using a more detailed sectoral classification,[5] this time in
terms of employment, shows a different picture for the
chemical industry in the United Kingdom, where 26.7 per
cent of employees are employed by multinationals. The
corresponding figure for France is 33.2 per cent. Other
industries show a degree of multinationalization as measured
by employment as follows:

	UK (%)	*France (%)*
Textiles and clothing	2.5	8.0
Pharmaceuticals	45.0	52.0 (of production)
Paper and allied trades	2.0	10.7
Basic industries	15.7	17.3

Multinationals and home country

The word 'multinational' is linked to the image of a foreign
enterprise. In the United Kingdom one thinks of Ford or
Michelin as multinationals rather than BL or Boots. The
latter two firms are, however, much more important for the
British economy than the North American and the French
giants mentioned. In Britain they only employ approximately

71 200 and 18 600 people respectively, whereas BL employs more than 143 300 and Boots 64 000 (see Table 3.1). These are good examples of the importance of the multinationals for the economies of their home countries. Before they established subsidiaries abroad, they were carrying on activities only in their own country. This nationwide activity did not stop when they became multinationals. Moreover, a large proportion of this home-based activity had to do with exports to the foreign subsidiaries. But the companies must acquire some dimension in their own country before investing abroad. Therefore, it can be assumed that:[6]

1. We find more multinationals among the very large firms than among the small and medium-sized firms.
2. The larger the firms are, the more their foreign operations represent a large share of their activities.

TABLE 2.3   *Share of Employment in Manufacturing Industry of Local Subsidiaries of Foreign Multinationals and Indigenous Multinationals*

Country	Number of employees in local subsidiaries of foreign multinationals % of total[a]	Number of employees in manufacturing industry in indigenous multinationals % of total[b]
USA	5.4 (1974)[c]	35 (1968)
Great Britain	12.4 (1975)	33 (1975)
Sweden	8.4 (1975)	34 (1976)
Germany	22.4 (1972)	40 (estimate)
Canada	43.1 (1974)	29 (1975)
France	19.0 (1975)	40 (estimate)

SOURCES

a. OECD, op. cit., p. 3.
b. International Labour Office, *Employment Effects of Multinational Enterprises in Industrialized Countries* (Geneva: ILO, 1981), p. 18.
    For Germany the figures comes from 33 firms. It underestimates the number of employees in the indigenous multinationals, but gives a ratio of 3/1 for them and the local subsidiaries of foreign firms.
c. Ibid., p. 7.

The indigenous multinationals are thus one of the most important economic agents for industry in their home country, always much more so than the local subsidiaries of the foreign multinationals. Table 2.3 shows this. It gives figures concerning the number of employees rather than the value added as the latter is not available for the indigenous multinationals. If we compare the first column of Table 2.1 and the first column of Table 2.3 we can see clearly that the two dimensions are very close and that more often than not the number of employees gives a very firm idea of the value added.

In large industrial countries like the United States, Canada or the United Kingdom, indigenous multinationals represent approximately one-third of the industrial activity of their home country. In Germany the rate is slightly higher, around 40 per cent. A similar rate probably applies to France. In Germany and France, firms sufficiently large to be competitive on a worldwide basis have taken a relatively larger share of the domestic economy than that taken in, say, the United States or the UK by multinationals of that country.

In small countries like Sweden, Holland or Switzerland, the percentage of employees in industry in the indigenous multinationals is also high. For these countries, this can be explained by the small size of the total national economy. To succeed, companies need to set up business abroad more quickly than those in larger countries like France or the United States.

GROWTH AND COMPETITION

Beginning at the end of the 1960s an idea had become strongly anchored in the images attached to multinationals, the belief that a decreasing number of multinationals would concentrate most of the economic power in the world in their hands before the year 2000. It is time now to look to see whether this is likely to happen.

Firstly, let us see whether the multinationals are taking a

growing share of the economies of the countries in which they are established, then, if they are, whether this growing share is taken by a smaller and smaller number of companies, a trend which would indicate increased concentration; and finally if the first fifty multinationals in the world have held their positions steady.

Growth of the multinationals[7]

The most precise way of measuring the growth of the multinationals would involve comparing the growth of the value added by the subsidiaries of the multinational firms with that of the gross domestic product of their host countries. Unfortunately, chronological series of these figures are not available, and Table 2.1 gives estimates for one year only.

Two other methods are available to express the growth of the multinationals in comparison with that of national economies. They give concordant results. The first compares the growth of the total of foreign direct investment worldwide with the growth of the gross national product in all the developed countries with market economies (from which nearly all of these investments come). Total, direct foreign investment grew at an average annual rate of 10.7 per cent from 1967 to 1971 and at 12.7 per cent from 1971 to 1976. During the same periods, the GNP of these countries increased 9.1 per cent and 13.5 per cent respectively.[8] The ratio of direct investment and gross national product therefore remained virtually unchanged from 1967 to 1976, increasing only from 6.7 to 6.9.[9] The direct investment of parent companies in their foreign subsidiaries, however, is only a small part of the local investment in the latter. In fact, they can borrow locally or reinvest their profits. Using the above figures involves the acceptance of the assumption that financing by the parent company's direct investments remains stable in relation to the other sources of financing. In reality, it would seem to be slightly on the decline, which gives credit to the thesis that the multinationals' economic importance in world terms is increasing slightly.

The second method of measuring growth consists of measuring the growth of employment due to the multinationals, in comparison with the growth of employment in their home countries and host countries. Later in the chapter on employment and the multinationals, it will be shown that this growth is either more rapid, or the same as the growth of industry in their home countries, and always more rapid than abroad.[10] Since the multinationals' share of world employment increases, their share of industrial production therefore increases.

The question arises here whether the increase in the multinational phenomenon is due to the growth of the older multinationals, or the entry of new ones. Taking the United Kingdom as an example, there was an increase in total foreign penetration in manufacturing in terms both of net output and employment between 1968 and 1977.[11] In 1968, 13.4 per cent of total output was from foreign-owned companies with USA-based companies dominating with 10.4 per cent. In employment, the figures were 9.7 per cent and 7.4 per cent respectively.

By 1977, the share of foreign-based multinationals in output and employment had both risen, but the share of USA-based companies had weakened in comparison with others. In output, the USA companies were taking only 13.1 per cent of the 19 per cent of total output represented by foreign-owned multinationals and 9.8 per cent of 13.9 per cent of employment, declines of 9.6 per cent and 8 per cent respectively over the decade. These figures would seem to suggest that any increase in multinationalization during the period in the United Kingdom came from the newer multinationals, particularly from other EEC countries as tariff barriers fell, rather than the older-established American groups. A similar trend is true of France.

The multinationals and concentration

If the multinationals are taking a growing share of industrial activity, is this share concentrated within the same number, or even of a declining number of firms?

Whatever the type of industry concerned, the answer is the same:

> . . . some industrial sectors, particularly older industries with economies of scale in production, are highly concentrated and have very few firms producing outside their country of origin. In those national markets where local production provides substantial advantages over importing, particularly if economies of scale in production are limited, a high degree of multinational participation may exist *with* [author's emphasis] a low degree of concentration. The tendency for multinational firms to follow each other into such industries has been noted.[12]

Thus, the best explanation for industrial concentration in a country depends on whether economies of scale in production are possible rather than whether firms are uninational or multinational. The best example is the iron and steel industry which, although declining and barely multinationalized, is very highly concentrated.

This observation is reinforced by the divergent evolution of the rate of industrial concentration and the participation of the multinationals in these sectors:

> The analysis of data for the United Kingdom and France tended to refute the theory that multinational operations and concentration were causally related. In neither country was there any trace of correlation between changes over time in the two variables. In the United Kingdom there was indeed a negative relationship between the level of foreign participation in each industry and changes in product concentration – over the two periods 1963–68 and 1968–75. Again, this correlation does not appear to be

causal: non-British firms are most strongly represented in expanding activities, and increases in concentration are generally associated with contraction.[13]

If the multinationals' share in industry grows, but existence of the multinational phenomenon is not the explanation for the growing rate of industrial concentration, the reason is not simply that these companies direct their activities toward sectors with a high rate of growth. It is also and especially because a growing number of uninational firms are investing abroad and so passing into the multinational category. As the number of multinationals – including small and medium-sized ones – is increasing relative to uninationals, the former naturally have a growing share of industrial activity. The millenarian vision of the world economy concentrated in the hands of a small number of multinationals (in the year 2000) is not in the least justified by the evolution of the phenomenon since the end of the Second World War.

This conclusion does not resolve what at first seems to be a paradox; the fact that multinationals have no impact on economic concentration in any given country does not at the same time stop a decline in the number of competitive companies on a world-wide basis. The automobile industry provides striking examples of this phenomenon. On the one hand, the number of companies of any significant size with manufacturing capacity in the United Kingdom has declined to three; BL, Ford and Vauxhall Motors (the United Kingdom subsidiary of General Motors of America), as BL has grown by mergers since its early days as the Austin Morris group to control of Rover, Jaguar and Leyland Motors, all of which were once independent companies. The trend in France has been similar where there are also now only two major manufacturing companies in the automobile industry – Renault and Peugeot-Citroën. At the end of the 1970s, Peugeot bought first Citroën and then Simca (the French subsidiary of Chrysler, the American company). Despite these developments, the number of competitors in the car industry in each country remains high. In fact, most automobile companies are represented in the main industrialized countries or rapidly industrializing countries, thanks to distribution and marketing subsidiaries. This is true not only of American companies present in Europe and Latin America, but also of the European ones, which spread out in the US and on other continents, and of Japanese companies, whose presence on world markets has blossomed spectacularly. World concentration and the growth of competition nationwide do not therefore constitute a paradox: they can and do coexist.

The top fifty multinationals

A comparative analysis of the identity of the fifty largest multinational groups in 1955 and 1975 is highly instructive.[14] The group of the 50 largest multinationals in the world can be divided into three subgroups:

1. The 23 companies which have remained at the top of the list – the 'Seven Sisters' oil companies; automobile manufacturers like Ford, General Motors or Chrysler; chemical manufacturers such as Dupont or ICI; or food industry companies (Nestlé, Unilever).
2. The 27 new companies which joined the top group – IBM, the electronic giant, prototype of the high technology firm; several European and Japanese companies, mostly in electronics, chemicals and automobiles; and two Third World oil companies: National Iran Oil and Petrobras (Brazil).
3. The 27 companies which are no longer in the top 50 group – five of them were absorbed into other groups, and the others simply fell to places lower down on the list. They are mainly aircraft manufacturers, steel manufacturers and companies making automobile accessories.

There are two explanations for these changes; the various industries in which the multinationals carry on their activities and the different countries in which they originate.

Thus from 1955 to 1975, the number of oil companies

within the top 50 group rose from 11 to 17; of electrical concerns from three to seven; and of chemicals manufacturers also from three to seven. There are now five steelmakers as opposed to six; nine manufacturers of mass consumer goods instead of four; and no aerospace equipment firms in the top 50, whereas in 1955 there were five of them.

If these changes are analysed in relation to the home countries of the multinationals in question it can be seen that, for the period from 1955 to 1975, the Western European companies increased their percentage in the top group from 28.5 per cent to 35.5 per cent; the Japanese went from 2.4 per cent to 9.9 per cent; companies from the developing countries from 8.8 per cent to 14.8 per cent; but American groups fell from 51.1 per cent to 37.2 per cent. This fall can be explained by the slowing down of the United States' rate of growth in relation to Europe after the Second World War and by the accelerated multinationalization of companies originating in Europe and Japan.

From a more general point of view:

> We could summarize the change over the two decades quite broadly, and very loosely, as a shift from an economy whose center of gravity was a World War II-type military industrial complex (motors, steel, aviation) to an economy in which the bulk of major firms and two-thirds of their sales is in the high technology field, with emphasis on oil, nuclear power, and computers.[15]

A top spot at present does not, therefore, guarantee the same classification in the future.

MULTINATIONALS IN RECESSION

The economic world changed for all companies and countries in 1974 following the massive increase in the oil price. The rapid expansion in the world's economy which had continued through the 1960s came to an abrupt end as the world plunged into recession. A second shock wave came after 1979 following another swingeing increase in oil prices.

There had been rapid growth in the world's economy between 1971 and 1973 after flexible exchange rates were introduced. It became relatively easy for countries to improve their growth rates simply by devaluing their currency. But recovery or booms based on exchange rate fluctuations can be very unstable, as proved to be the case in the aftermath of the oil shock; with growth came massive rises in commodity and property prices. The bubble burst with the oil shock. In 1974 and 1975, average GNP worldwide actually fell. The recovery which was underway by the end of the 1970s ended in 1980 with the second wave of oil price rises.

It is especially difficult to discuss or estimate direct foreign investment trends during this period and, it follows, the effect of the recession on the operations of multinationals. It will be some time before complete research into performance during this period can be collated and assessed. Such figures that are so far available show quite conclusively[16] that direct foreign investment in stocks and flows rose between 1967 and 1971, eased back between 1971 and 1975 and then picked up again between 1975 and 1980. Within this overall picture, however, the attitude of companies varied from country to country and from sector to sector.

A sample of the world's largest industrial companies[17] showed that their average return on assets was 5.8 per cent in 1962, falling to 4.1 per cent by 1972, but recovering to 5.1 per cent by 1977, suggesting that the 1974–75 setback had little, if any effect on absolute profit levels. However, interest rates increased more than firms' profits showing a relative decline in the latter. Furthermore, companies had divested themselves of unprofitable subsidiaries. Again, direct investment flows as a percentage of fixed capital formation for 11 developed countries show very little change in the 20 years from 1960 to 1980. In 1960–62 it was 2.7 per cent and for 1978–80 had risen only to 2.9 per cent.[18]

So one must turn elsewhere to try to assess what changes, if any have occurred in the operations of multinationals during the recession. There are few statistics to serve as a guide and, at best, any conclusions must be highly tentative and subject to enormous variation between companies, sectors and countries. It can be said that so far there are no trends discernible which are common to all multinationals. The main question to be answered is whether there has been an increase or a decrease in multinationalization as a result of the recession. Increased multinationalization can follow from one or both of the following two factors:

1. Indigenous multinationals in one country increase their competitive position in world markets and therefore increase their international operations, or;
2. The attractiveness of local investment overseas increases.

Clearly, these factors can apply whether any economy or the world's economy is in a phase of growth or recession. During the 1980–82 setback at least, neither factor appears to have emerged strongly. In Europe as a whole, multinational operations do not appear to be growing. There has indeed been some evidence of disinvestment abroad by both American and European companies. Arguments have been put forward that multinational companies are more likely to cease the operations of their foreign subsidiaries rather than their home-based activities, if they have any choice.[19] Unemployment at home is often cited as a major reason and empirical evidence suggests that it is certainly a factor. The automobile companies are typical. BL, the British-based car company, is pulling out of its Belgian operation and the French PSA-Peugeot-Citroën group, too, has closed down its Chrysler plant which it bought from the Americans in the late 1970s. In a uninational company, the relatively unprofitable branches are the first to go in a recession. In an international context, this can mean the ending of operations in an entire country.

It might be expected, too, that a recession would lead to concentration in industry both on a national and international level, but this does not necessarily seem to be the case. In the United Kingdom, for example, before 1968, there were signs of increasing concentration in industry, but not in those sectors where foreign companies were present. The concentration which took place then was mainly through defensive mergers between uninational companies, and in those sectors where foreign multinationals were important, competition increased. In the decade to 1968, the concentration ratios in the 125 industries in the United Kingdom were 38 per cent. These rose to 48–9 per cent in the next ten years[20] and there appears to have been a decline since, though it will be some time before the statistical evidence can be measured.

Such evidence as is so far available illustrates the difficulties in predicting companies' actions and attitudes in industries where there is temporary or permanent over-capacity. One thing which does not appear to happen in recession is any decline in competition. Fishwick reaches a tentative conclusion:

. . . there appears to have been intensive competition not only through advertising, but also through product innovations and prices. It is too early yet to draw definite and quantified conclusions from the event of recent months, but there are indications that this competition has been intensified by its international character.[21]

3 The Role of the Multinationals in the Economy

This chapter will attempt to answer three questions. What is the role of the multinationals in the economies of their home and host countries? What importance do they have for the world economy? And what is their role in economic development?

THEIR PLACE IN NATIONAL ECONOMIES

We will examine successively the role that the multinationals play in relation to employment and inflation.

EMPLOYMENT

It may seem surprising but it is nevertheless a fact that statistics comparing the numbers of jobs in the world by country and industrial sector, with a breakdown for jobs furnished by foreign multinationals, indigenous multinationals, uninationals and governments, do not exist. As it is, it is necessary to fall back on estimates. One of the closest estimates of the total number of employees (salaried workers in the world) puts the figure at 440 million,[1] with a corresponding total for those employed by multinationals, both foreign and indigenous, at 46 million.[2] This latter figure is probably an underestimate and it seems likely that multinationals represent between 10 and 15 per cent of employment in those parts of the world in which they can carry on activities. This is certainly less than the total number employed by the governments of the different countries.[3] Nevertheless, their role is much more important in the developed countries which are members of the Organization for Economic Cooperation and Development (OECD), than in the developing countries. In the former, multinationals employ 42 million out of a total of 275 000 000 salaried workers[5] or 15.3 per cent.[6] In the developing countries, in contrast, multinationals only employ four million persons out of 175 million salaried workers[7] or 2.3 per cent.[8]

As Table 2.3 showed, this employment is concentrated in manufacturing in the industrialized countries. The participation of the multinationals there varies from between 40 per cent and 70 per cent of local employment. The indigenous multinationals employ three times as many in each country as the local subsidiaries of foreign multinationals.

Table 3.1 illustrates this phenomenon in the United Kingdom: of the top 30 British employers, 18 are British multinationals, with one, Unilever, under joint Anglo-Dutch control, only two, Ford Motor and George Weston, who rank eighteenth and nineteenth are foreign multinationals, and 10 uninationals, of which all but one are nationalized concerns.

It is interesting to observe that, of the ten state-controlled firms only one is a multinational (BL). The nine state-controlled employers are all uninationals, though British Steel was formerly a multinational. In France, the situation is almost reversed.[9] Table 3.1 leaves out major British multinationals like British Petroleum, Shell, British American Tobacco or Rio Tinto. Indeed these firms have a relatively small number of employees in Great Britain as compared with their large world-wide total. These companies were incorporated about a century ago. They had time to develop their overseas subsidiaries considerably while their industry was not prone to large domestic growth. This is quite typical of many British multinationals which relied on their foreign operations to sustain a rate of growth which the British economy alone could not have permitted. In the case of American, German or French multinationals one does not

TABLE 3.1   *Britain's Top 30 Employers*[a]

Rank	Company	Type	Main Activity	No. of Employees UK	No. of Employees Foreign
1.	*National Coal Board* [e]	U	coal mining	296 000	—
2.	British Telecom	U	telephones, telecommunications	245 000	—
3.	*British Rail* [e]	U	railway services	212 730	—
4.	*The Post Office* [e]	U	postal services	178 038	—
5.	*Electricity Council* [e]	U	electricity suppliers	154 910	—
6.	General Electric	IM	electrical and electronic engineers	145 346	43 456 [b]
7.	*British Gas* [e]	U	gas suppliers	117 900	—
8.	*British Leyland* [e]	IM	automobile manufacturers	114 660	28 664
9.	Grand Metropolitan	IM	brewers, hotels, milk products	103 129	28 628
10.	Imperial Group	IM	tobacco, food, drink	82 400	40 000 [c]
11.	*British Steel* [e]	U	steel products	80 000	—
12.	THORN EMI	IM	electrical and electronic engineers	78 083	19 442
13.	National Westminster Bank	IM	bankers	77 000	10 000
14.	Barclays Bank	IM	bankers	76 000	44 000
15.	British Aerospace	IM	aircraft manufacturers	75 520	3 669 [c]
16.	Imperial Chemical Industries	IM	chemicals, fibres	74 700	57 700 [b]
17.	Unilever	IM [d]	food products, detergents	73 252	218 748
18.	Ford Motor	FM	automobile manufacturer	71 700·	333 088
19.	George Weston	FM	food manufacturers & distributors	74 114	39 000
20.	Bass	IM	brewers	69 456	2 778
21.	Allied Lyons	IM	brewers, hoteliers	64 509	11 100
22.	Boots	IM	manufacturing, wholesale & retail chemists	63 886	5 879
23.	Courtaulds	IM	man-made fibres	62 636	17 346 [c]
24.	*London Transport* [e]	U	public transport services	59 879	—
25.	*National Bus Company* [e]	U	public bus services	53 172	—
26.	Lucas Industries	IM	vehicle and aircraft components	53 003	18 538
27.	Lloyds Bank	IM	bankers	52 117	28 112
28.	Sears Holdings	IM	footwear, stores, engineering	51 000	6 000
29.	Midland Bank	IM	bankers	50 785	18 247
30.	Tesco	U	supermarkets	49 610	—

SOURCES Companies, company accounts; Margaret Allen (ed.), *The Times 1000, 1982–3* (London: Times Books). J. M. Stopford, *The World Directory of Multinational Enterprises, 1982–3* (London: Macmillan).

NOTES
a. Not including direct government employees.
b. Average weekly total of employees.
c. Total at year-end.
d. Anglo-Dutch control.
e. Companies in *italic* are all state or publicly-owned utilities or corporations.

U = uninational; IM = indigenous multinational; FM = foreign multinational.

find such outstanding examples. Most large multinationals are amongst the top employers in their country of origin.

Within the general context of an increase in employment in manufacturing from the Second World War up until 1973 and a decline since then, it is important to know whether multinationals slow down, or accentuate this phenomenon. They are frequently blamed in all the industrialized countries for exporting jobs abroad, particularly to countries with cheap labour. Nevertheless, the conclusions in this area seem to go against such commonly held beliefs:

> The available data, including those from a special ILO survey undertaken among a sample of more than 250 major Australian, Canadian, European and Japanese MNEs, indicate that, in approximately the last 10–15 years, employment in foreign operations of MNEs has generally tended to grow more rapidly than in their home country operations, such increases being most marked in the developing host countries .... At the same time, where such information was available for the same period, it has been found that the employment trends of MNEs in their main industrialized home countries has, on the whole, been broadly in line with the general trend in manufacturing. At times MNE employment increases were even greater than the general increases in employment, such as in the United States, the Federal Republic of Germany, the United Kingdom, Switzerland and Sweden ... the foreign employment expansion of multinational enterprises was thus not accompanied, over the longer-term period of the last 10–15 years, by a decrease in the employment volume in the home country operations. Therefore, the hypothesis of a large-scale 'employment export' by these enterprises – understood here in the (limited) sense of a corresponding fall in the volume of domestic employment associated with the expansion of the volume of employment in MNE operations abroad – is not confirmed by the finding of this study, for the period and countries considered.[10]

In France for a much shorter period (from 1974 to 1977) a sample of 67 French firms confirmed more rapid growth of employment abroad than in France.[11] The global figure for total employed manpower in France also increased. Once growth by acquisition by some of these firms in French territory is eliminated, however, sector-by-sector analysis showed a decline of employment in France and an increase abroad in the majority of the sectors and for a majority of the firms.[12]

It is very difficult to evaluate the impact the multinationals would have had on employment, if they had not increased their foreign investments. J. Savary has shown clearly that the foreign subsidiaries of the French multinationals are an important element in their competitive strength in exports[13] and so the foreign subsidiaries partly keep the French factories working. That would probably have been the case, but to a lesser extent, if they had not increased their activities abroad. The effect on national employment would perhaps have been even more negative.

If indigenous multinationals increase employment abroad to a greater extent than they do in their home countries, it means that, for each host country for international investment, foreign firms participate in the increase of local employment. The global effect of the multinationals (indigenous and foreign) on employment in a given country seems therefore, to be either more positive or less negative than that of uninational firms in the same country. Because they spread their risks over several countries and because they are willing to exploit the most sophisticated technologies and markets, it is not illogical that multinationals are often more profitable and more resistant to economic slowdowns and worker layoffs than uninational companies.

This evolution has been illustrated by a case study of foreign investments in Belgium.[14] Between 1968 and 1975 the local subsidiaries of foreign companies created 80 000 jobs (110 000 new jobs less 30 000 jobs eliminated), or an annual rate of growth of 5.1 per cent. During the same period, Belgian industry as a whole lost 30 544 jobs (a 0.43 per cent annual rate of decline). Then from 1975 to 1978 the growth in employment from the subsidiaries of foreign groups declined, reducing the annual rate of growth to 0.14 per cent, compared with a rate of decline of 3.97 per cent for all Belgian industry. The fear of a massive withdrawal of foreign investments due to the crisis did not materialize. Globally speaking, the increase in employment from the local subsidiaries of the foreign multinationals was greater than the decline in employment in the indigenous activities of the Belgian multinationals.

It is wrong to conclude, however, that multinationals have the reverse effect and play a part in reducing unemployment. In fact, as already noted, they are essentially concentrated in manufacturing, a sector in which total employment is on the decline. Many economies are now in a post-industrial phase[15] in which the service industries are playing a growing part. Within the service sector, government services are by far the principal employer and create more jobs than private companies, multinational or not.

INFLATION

Because of the competition between them in all the countries in which they are active, multinational companies must be very attentive to the evolution of their cost prices (costs). To this end, they look for the cheapest and most reliable sources of supply.

As a result, multinational companies are an important element in the search for efficiency and the minimization of costs on an international level. By importing in a given country from another country with lower production costs, the multinationals contribute to a lower rate of inflation in the importing country. It is, however, difficult to put figures to this phenomenon. Above and beyond the supplies coming from other companies, multinationals can try to produce themselves. They would do this in countries which have the greatest advantages in their particular sector, in order to supply all or part of the sales or marketing subsidiaries. Such factories are known as shop subsidiaries. There are relatively few of them and they exist only in certain industries like textiles where the role of production abroad is negligible.[16]

On the other hand, to ensure the stability of supply to their markets and the quality of their products, multinationals must avoid the risk of strikes and maintain good relations with the unions. At the same time, they often agree to pay their employees a little more than the other firms to attract and keep a highly dependable labour force.[17] So they are left 'in peace'. For those multinationals whose production is integrated world-wide, a strike or a series of low quality products could mean a loss of their share of the market in several countries at the same time, because a single factory can easily supply several countries. The conclusion must be that multinationals participate in the increasing of costs and therefore, it follows, of inflation. In this way, their behaviour is exactly analogous with that of the government, which is the biggest employer in the large industrialized countries. A recent study made by the OECD[18] attributes inflation to the bad habit of governments of tolerating larger and larger budget deficits. Governments' logic is, in fact, the same as that of companies: it is easier to increase the budget deficit, which can be financed through loans, than decrease costs by resisting the demands for budget increases which come from the different ministries – too many civil servants and certain professional categories would be displeased if such a course were adopted. Plainly speaking, it is easier to borrow money to pay for wage increases than to say no to several million salaried workers, especially if that could lead to a defeat at the next General Election. It is the very nature of all large, complex organizations to feed inflation, whether this is done negatively or positively. It is clear then that multinationals participate on the one hand in lowering inflation, but on the other in raising it, but there are no statistics in this area which allow any calculation of the proportion of the former in relation to the latter. As the tendency to lower costs through a worldwide rationalization of the sources of supply of finished or semi-finished goods only holds for a part of the multinationals' activity (a large share of their output is sold locally) and whereas the tendency to want to be 'left in peace' (or to recompense their workers and employees) holds for the whole of their activities, the global impact of the multinationals is probably on balance slightly inflationary.

IMPORTANCE IN THE WORLD ECONOMY

Let us now go on to examine successively the importance of the role of the multinationals in international trade, the rates of exchange, and the balance of payments.

INTERNATIONAL TRADE

Over the years, except for the years 1975 and 1981, the growth of international trade has been larger than the general growth of the gross national product of the various countries. Table 3.2 shows that from 1963 to 1968 world production increased at an annual rate of 6.4 per cent, and from 1973 to 1978 at an annual rate of 3.5 per cent. During the same periods, the volume of international trade increased at an annual rate of 8.3 per cent and 4.2 per cent.

TABLE 3.2   *Comparative Evolution of the Growth of Production and of Exports in the World (annual rate of progression in percentages)*

	1963–68	1968–73	1973–78
World production (volume)	6.4	5.8	3.5
World exports	8.3	9.2	4.2

SOURCE   A. Bavelier, *Le commerce extérieur* (Foreign Trade) (Paris: PUF, 'Que sais-je?' Collection, 1980), p. 23.

This means that in the United Kingdom, for example, the relative share of British production destined for export increases at the same time as the British consume an increased share of imported goods, or, for 1980, 29.1 per cent.[19] At the same time as BL exports more cars the British buy an increasing number of Japanese or German cars.

This phenomenon has become more and more important since the Second World War and the market economy countries have never before reached such a high degree of interdependence. The phenomenon has been an important driving force for growth, for it has caused an increase in demand and a greater diversification of goods.

What part of this international trade comes from multinational companies (transactions between the parent company and the subsidiaries or inter-subsidiary)? Once again, this is difficult to evaluate, in this case because the multinationals' internal transactions can be basically of three types:

1. As far as raw materials are concerned, Chapter 1 showed that the multinationals' share is declining in favour of local companies. Thus transactions increasingly represent trade between different firms.
2. In manufacturing, these transactions may deal with finished products; the subsidiaries then work as importing agents, a situation which would have no impact on international trade. If the parent companies are not competitive, subsidiaries can always buy elsewhere.
3. On the other hand, there is a series of transactions in manufacturing which deals with intermediate goods, which illustrates worldwide integration of the organization of production. This has been the case, for example, in the automobile industry since the beginning of the 1980s. Such transactions clearly influence the flow of international trade. When this happens, international trade no longer depends solely on the comparative advantages of countries, but also on the worldwide organization of production by the multinationals in these sectors.

This means, on balance, that while the share of the multinationals in international trade has been declining as far as raw materials are concerned, there has been an increase in their share of total manufacturing output. Globally speaking, nevertheless, the share of the multinationals in international trade is growing.[20] Thus, in 1977, approximately 48 per cent of American imports resulted from internal transactions of the multinationals with 24 per cent (as against only 20 per cent in 1973) coming from American companies importing from their own foreign subsidiaries. The remaining 24 per cent came from the exports of foreign-based multinationals to their subsidiaries in the United States. As for American exports, in 1970, 50 per cent came from internal transactions of the multinationals.[21]

The same information for Great Britain and Sweden gives 30 per cent in 1973 and 29 per cent in 1975 respectively of exports from the multinationals' internal transactions.[22]

Unfortunately, it is not known what part of these transactions represent semi-finished products. The statistics to hand[23] show, however, that in 1975, 59 per cent of the merchandise exported by some hundred sample American companies was in finished goods, an increase from the figure of 53 per cent for the same firms in 1970. During the same period, the proportion of finished goods in imports fell to 59 per cent from 65 per cent in 1970. As for imports of raw materials, they rose from 9 per cent to 15 per cent of the total. Intermediate goods represented 25 per cent of the merchandise imported in 1975 by the sample companies in the United States.

RATES OF EXCHANGE

The rate of exchange measures one currency in terms of another: for example, on 31 December 1982, the pound sterling changed hands at $1.62 or, put another way, 61.7 pence were needed to buy each dollar. Only a month later on 31 January 1983, the rate of the pound sterling had fallen to $1.52. This meant that 65.8 pence were then needed to buy each dollar, a 6 per cent decline in the value of sterling over one month.

A fall in the value of one currency against another has important economic effects for the country whose currency has fallen in value, whether this results from an actual devaluation, or merely a fall through market forces. There is a medium-term positive effect on commercial transactions with other countries. For example, if the rate of exchange of sterling falls, British goods will be sold at lower prices abroad and will be more competitive. The lower value of the pound sterling will therefore have a positive effect on the commercial balance of the United Kingdom, all the more so in that at the same time the foreign goods sold in Britain will be more expensive, and less competitive. On the other hand, the investments of the British companies abroad will have become dearer at the same time as the foreign investments in Britain become cheaper. This means that a fall in the value of the pound would handicap the British multinationals in any financing of investments abroad from the head office. Further, when currency devalues, foreign goods, which become more expensive, contribute to increases in the retail price index and so fuel inflation.

The devaluation of a country's currency, therefore, has positive and negative effects. It is considered as negative, however, even if it does aid exports and, it follows, employment. This is because of the very great danger in the long term which a high rate of inflation represents for the economy of any country. But there is also national pride involved in the desire to maintain a country's exchange rate. Strong currencies are admired and favoured, probably because the strongest economies, such as those of the United States, West Germany or Switzerland, have the strongest currencies. This explains why any economic agent participating in the devaluation of the country's currency has a bad reputation.

The belief that multinationals are such agents underlies the reproaches frequently directed at them. They are thought to provoke the fall of the currency of their home base and to work to this end by speculations in the foreign exchange market, the international market dealing with currency exchange.

Companies can indeed intervene in several positive ways and affect the rate of exchange as a result. They can do this firstly through their international trade operations – exports and imports; secondly, by using their international investment operations; and lastly, by investing their available funds on a short term basis to obtain a higher rate of interest than that prevailing in their country.

What, precisely, are the possibilities for speculation within these three types of activity?

(1) *International trade*

Let us take the example of a British company working with Germany and billing its exports in Deutsche Marks. The company, in order to repatriate its Deutsche Marks, can theoretically wait for the rate of this currency to go up and so improve its profits. If the rate of exchange of the pound to the DM falls from DM 4.0 to 3.80, the British business will have made an extra margin of five per cent in relation to the rate of the pound sterling. This company, whether a uni- or multi-national, will have speculated on a rise of the DM. By so doing, it has participated in a fall in the value of the pound sterling in relation to the DM.

Imagine the opposite case: that of a British company importing goods from Germany. Facing a foreseeable rise of the Deutsche Mark it will hurry to pay right away, offering on the foreign exchange market the pound sterling. This action will automatically lead to the pound falling in relation to the DM. The possibility of changing the terms involved in exchange is called using the 'leads and lags'. British companies are free to buy and sell whatever currencies they wish and can influence rates of exchange in this way. In contrast, companies in some other countries, where exchange control is imposed, are not free to operate in the foreign exchange market. French companies, for example, cannot buy foreign currency as they like. Any purchase must correspond to a commercial or financial transaction because of very strict controls on exchange. All transactions are dealt with by a banking intermediary nominated by the Banque de France to check that exchange control regulations are adhered to.

Moreover, most French companies bill their customers abroad in their own currency, the French franc. Their practice is not unusual: British firms bill mainly in sterling and American firms in US dollars. This means that they cannot deal in the foreign exchange market. If, by chance, they do bill in foreign currencies, they have usually already sold them in forward sales to their bank and, therefore, cannot change their minds and go in for foreign exchange speculation.[24] Lastly, the regulations on exchange control requires French companies to repatriate foreign currency two weeks at the latest after being paid by their clients.[25] It severely limits the time they would have available for currency speculation. This is not true in Britain, however, as foreign exchange controls were abolished by the Thatcher Government.

Moreover, the risks of gains and losses taken by companies when speculating on rates of exchange are not symmetrical; taking a risk to make a gain implies that there is also the risk of a loss. The gain may be commendable, as it increases the profitability of the company, but the loss may put its survival in danger. When a manager speculates and makes a gain, his financial manager may congratulate him, but he will be warned of the risks. Lastly, as far as management costs are concerned, it is important to remember that all speculation involves rather heavy costs: the salaries of highly-paid executives and consultants.

(2) *Investments*

As investments are specific operations, they are relatively rare occurrences in the life of a company. They depend on the opportunities which come along and which must be taken advantage of quickly. This means that it is difficult to speculate on international investments.

(3) *Cash management*

Very often the only way for a firm to speculate is to place its short-term cash for a few days in a foreign currency whose value is likely to rise in a short while. This type of foreign currency, however, is often a strong or 'hard' currency which offers lower interest than other currencies. A company could of course also borrow weak or 'soft' currency for several days, then convert it into hard currency and later still reimburse its loan in 'soft' currency once the latter had fallen. Such operations as this are relatively rare, because speculation in this way is expensive and risky. Indeed, borrowing weak currencies about which there are rumours of a fall reach astronomical rates of interest on the international capital market: they may be as high as 300 per cent.

Moreover, in order to carry out these operations, the firms must have the right to buy foreign currency without any matching transaction. As shown above, it is impossible for companies in countries with foreign exchange controls, like France, Belgium or Italy to operate in this way. On the other hand, the companies originating in countries like Britain, the USA or Germany where there is no such control can, as we have seen, speculate on the international market. Nevertheless, these operations by companies represent only 10 per cent of the operations on the foreign exchange market and the remaining 90 per cent are autonomous operations by banks.

Exchange rates on the foreign markets are established by the banks and not by companies. The rate of exchange in general follows the differences in the rate of interest between countries more or less closely. In a country with a high rate of interest (usually associated with a high rate of inflation), the currency will fall, or be devalued in relation to the countries where the rate of interest is lower. For example, if Britain has an average annual rate of interest of 10 per cent and Germany 5 per cent, the pound sterling will lose 5 per cent of its value in relation to the Deutsche Mark each year. The speculatory movements on the foreign exchange market are caused by the deals of the banks' specialist exchange brokers at the time when they readjust the rates of exchange of these currencies.

THE BALANCE OF PAYMENTS

The balance of payments is an accounting tool which measures all the transactions between the residents of one country and those of other countries for a given period, generally speaking one year. The balance of payments, therefore, records flows and not stocks. A company just like a resident can very well be of a nationality other than that of the country in which it operates. For example: the movements of money abroad during a given period made by a subsidiary of an American company established in Britain are recorded in the British balance of payments just like those of a British resident, since this subsidiary has British legal status.

The balance of payments of each country is recorded in its own currency by the central bank.

The balance of payments is divided essentially into two parts: the trade balance, which details the imports and exports of goods and services, as well as their balance; and the balance of financial operations which gives the balance and details of the investment and portfolio transactions made by individuals, companies, banks and the governments with foreign countries. It is this part which permits us to know the annual total of British investments abroad and of foreign investments in Britain.

Thus, trade transactions have to do with exchanges of tangible goods and services, and financial transactions with exchanges of monies, securities and properties.

All exports improve the balance of payments since they bring foreign currency into the country; all imports in contrast lower the balance of payments since they imply an outflow of currency to another country. In the same way, British direct investment abroad depresses the balance of financial operations, whereas the foreign investments in Britain improve it. Adding together the trade balance and the balance of financial operations gives the overall total balance of payments.

The question which now arises is, what impact if any do the multinationals have on the balance of payments?

The answer in the industrialized countries is that their impact is difficult to measure, since one is generally dealing with cross-investments of the United States in Europe, and vice-versa. However, one can assume that the United States, the country whose firms have the most important investment abroad will have generally speaking a negative impact on the balance of payments of the host countries in which its multinationals operate because, rather than using direct investment, most of the time American companies raise money locally. For example, when the British subsidiary of the American computer company, IBM, increases its investments in Britain, it tends to borrow on the local or international banking market rather than borrowing from its American head office. This type of local loan is a transaction between two British residents and is therefore not registered in the balance of payments. But since the volume of activity and (probably) profits of IBM in Britain will increase, the subsidiary will eventually repatriate more money to the United States, where the head office is located and this transaction will show as an outflow in the British balance of payments. Since direct foreign investment to the developed countries is low because the multinationals generally use local borrowing, the activities of the multinationals there have a more negative effect on the balance of payments than they do in the developing countries. In those countries the multinationals rarely have access to local loans and must export capital from their home base if they want to invest there.

Most of the types of accounts above relate only to financial operations in the balance of payments; the most important part, trade operations, is often forgotten. In the preceding example, the balance of exports from the factories of IBM in Britain, in relation to its imports coming from the factories of its sister subsidiaries in other European countries is several times larger than the profit repatriated to the United States.

Another recent example, also involving IBM, though it does not invalidate the above over the long-term, shows how a multinational can, through a policy decision, favourably affect one country's balance of payments at the expense of another. When IBM won the £15 million contract in Britain for the Swansea Driver & Vehicle Licensing Centre, it was widely expected that the computer would be built in the United Kingdom. IBM United Kingdom Ltd had spent some time persuading the British Government that it was a British firm and that it could increase jobs in the country, if it were not regarded as a foreigner. Having gained the contract, however, the company announced it would be building the computer in France – to the immediate detriment of the British balance of payments and to the benefit of the French.

The next question which needs to be answered is, what is the impact of the multinationals on the balance of payment of a given host country? A specific example will give us an idea of this.[26]

From 1965–68 in Latin America, American multinationals invested 700 million dollars, but at the same time their subsidiaries repatriated $1440 million of profit back to the USA. This meant that for these Latin American countries there was a net deficit of $740 million in the balance of payments. During the same period, however, the American subsidiaries in Latin America were responsible for $4.5 billion exports. If we add to the above figure $4.8 billion representing the estimated import substitutions, where the local production by the foreign subsidiaries made the import of certain goods unnecessary, the net benefit to the balance of payments of the Latin American countries becomes $9.3 billion for the period 1965–68.

This example shows clearly that numerous variables must be included in the calculation of the impact of the multinationals on the balance of payments of the host countries. Their net impact for all operations appears to be globally positive in the short run. In the long run, the net effect depends on the capacity of locally-based companies themselves to create the type of activities engendered by the subsidiaries of the foreign multinationals. It follows that the governments of the host countries most often insist on having the multinationals invest in their countries and create factories, even if at first it increases the cost of local production in relation to imports. For a government, it is advantageous over the longer term to create local industry, on the condition that it develops and its products become, in the end, cheaper than imports. One must not forget, too, that in case of shortage or war, it is always important to have factories at one's disposal!

The final question here is what is the impact of the multinationals on the balance of payments of their home country? Two studies give the same answer for the United States and Great Britain.[27] In the short term the effect is a negative one because there is a fall in exports, but in the long term the effect is positive, because of the exports which follow local investment and the repatriation of dividends. If the impact of the multinationals of a country on the balance of payments of both their home and their host countries can be positive in the two cases, it means that we are not dealing with a zero sum gain. New investments create new activities. What is more, multinationals alone represent less than half of the transactions recorded in the balance of payments.

ROLE IN ECONOMIC DEVELOPMENT

We will now examine successively the transfer of technology and transfer prices.

TRANSFER OF TECHNOLOGY

The transfer of technology is the sale, in this case by a multinational, of a technique and the means of using it and above all the training of personnel. If the sale is made to a subsidiary, it is an internal or intra-company transfer. If it is made to a firm outside the group, it is an external transfer.

Historically speaking, the transfers of technology made by

the multinational firms were a means for the transferees to catch up economically speaking to the transferors. The British companies at the turn of the century and, even more so, the Americans after the Second World War were not simply exporting capital when they were developing their activities abroad: they also exported management capabilities and technology. That permitted the host countries to develop their technology and catch up little by little, in particular with the USA. This catching up – mainly by the countries of Western Europe and Japan – is said to have accelerated the relative decline of the American multinationals.[28]

Gilpin's thesis is clear:

> . . . not that the relative decline of the American economy has been due principally to foreign direct investment; nor is it that this relative decline was somehow avoidable. Powerful economic forces beyond the control of the United States have accounted for this shift in the locus of industrial power. But certainly foreign direct investment has been a contributing factor in that it has accelerated the process and has inhibited . . . a rejuvenation of the American economy.[29]

If the American and British multinationals had not set up subsidiaries abroad there would not have been intracompany transfers of technology. But the external transfers could not have been stopped: the foreign companies would most likely have bought patents, licences and the means of using them. The catching up with the United States and Great Britain would still have happened, but perhaps a bit more slowly.

The above reasoning, made for the transferors of technology to the transferees, permits the conclusion that it is in the interest of the latter to accept transfers of technology, especially if the countries in question are developing ones, so that they can catch up with the industrialized countries. In the same way, the countries which want to develop their advanced technology industries to the maximum should establish subsidiaries of their companies in countries where these technologies are indeed the most advanced and where demand is directed toward the most sophisticated products. For example, in order to develop the newest electronic equipment, the specialized British or French firms should buy subsidiaries on the West Coast of the United States rather than developing their activities solely within Britain or France.

Once again, it is difficult to measure the extent of the phenomenon of transfer of technology because the prices of these transfers include more than the royalties on the patents. Management contracts, the cost of the intermediate goods linked to the transfer, which are exported whether the transfers are internal or external, as well as other parameters difficult to measure must also be included. Evaluating the evolution of the transfer of technology by measuring only patent royalties does not permit more than a broad idea of the importance of the phenomenon and its evolution.

For example, in 1973 the United States had net receipts (receipts minus payments) of $2.6 billion[30] in royalties and by 1980, $6.2 billion.[31] To get an idea of the dimension of these figures they can be compared with those of United States exports for the same years: $70 billion in 1973 and $216.6 billion in 1980,[32] or 4.6 per cent and 2.8 per cent respectively.

In 1980, 85 per cent of these net royalties was due to the activity of the multinationals with their foreign subsidiaries ($5.2 billion) and only 15 per cent to the exporting of technology by American companies not established abroad ($0.9 billion).[31]

A comparison can be made with the United Kingdom. In 1973 total net receipts, patents and royalties were £41.7 million, and in 1980, £119.3 million whereas the exports for these two years went from £17.71 billion to £148.45 billion.[33] But the relative share of the British multinationals is not available.

As far as the influence of the transfer of technology by the multinationals on the developing countries goes, these countries are torn between two apparently contradictory objectives: controlling their own industrial technology and accelerating their development. At the centre of this contradiction is an intellectual debate.

On one side are the partisans of appropriate technology,[34] tailor-made for the particular need of the country concerned; it must avoid any brutal break with the traditional social or cultural environment; it is more labour- than capital-intensive and leads to the creation of more jobs than does more advanced technology.

On the other side, there is the argument put forward by A. Emmanuel,[35] which favours the introduction of the most advanced technology. His argument can be summarized in three points:

1. The most capital-intensive technology, that is, the most recent, maximizes the quantity of goods available to the population, therefore, maximizing social welfare.
2. The transfer of the most advanced technology helps to accelerate the development of the most highly industrialized countries and constitutes a short-cut in closing the 'technology gap' between the industrialized countries and the Third World. According to the author, those who favour only technology appropriate to current local conditions perpetrate underdevelopment and misery in a permanent way.
3. Since advanced technology is in the hands of the multinationals, they become the privileged vehicle of the technological shortcut for the Third World.

What happens in reality? Do the governments of the developing countries demand appropriate technology, or the most advanced technology? In general, the state-controlled companies of these host countries require the most advanced technology. When older technology is proposed to them, they often have the impression that they are victims of a sort of racism, that they are considered buyers of obsolete, pollution-causing technologies. This attitude prevails to such an extent that certain countries, for example, Algeria, require by contract the most advanced technology, even if it means stopping payment of royalties if it is proved that they have been misled about what they are buying.

There are other countries like India which vary their response according to the industry in question: 'pauperized' technology in the automobile industry, is one example. In 1953, the Draconian conditions imposed by the Indian government meant that Ford and General Motors ceased operations there. Today, the Indians manufacture models from the fifties – Morris Oxford, Fiat 1100 and Triumph Herald.[36] In contrast, when it comes to defence, the Indians want the most advanced technology to equip their army. Thus the USSR (Migs) competed with France (Mirages) to supply their fighter planes.

Within the international agencies, the developing countries demand that transfers of technology be made to them free of charge. Thus they do not negotiate the type of technology but the price of the most advanced technology. Their arguments are simple: since those transferring the technology have already redeemed the price of Research and Development at home, there is no reason for the purchaser to pay that price a second time in the form of royalties. The multinationals response is that they need the royalties to finance the Research and Development of future technologies, and these are becoming increasingly expensive.

With a view to their own development, the important thing is that the technology be transferred efficiently, meaning that the host countries be able to put it into practice. What must be avoided – although it has sometimes been the case – is the creation of what are truly factory ghost towns. In fact, the price of the transfer of technology is not the most important element of the question.

TRANSFER PRICES

It would seem logical for multinational companies (like uninationals, moreover) to try to maximize their profits. The minimization of taxation is one of the means among many of so doing. Multinationals appear to be well organized to be able to carry out this operation by means of transfer prices, that is, the prices at which the parent company sells its products to its subsidiaries, or those used between sister subsidiaries. One of the criticisms frequently made of multinationals is that they manipulate transfer prices and thus manage to concentrate their profit in those countries in which they operate where they face the lowest taxes.

Obviously, no empirical study permits the measurement of the frequency of such manipulations. Naturally, however, it is easier to do where the company in question is the sole supplier of the merchandise and where there would therefore be no reference to a market price. It would still be necessary to hoodwink the taxation authorities in each of the countries in which the multinational is carrying on activities – and the interests of these different countries are generally divergent. Moreover, multinationals achieve the largest proportion of their turnover in industrialized countries like the United States, Europe and Japan where the tax rates are relatively similar. In tax havens like the Bahamas and Liberia, the multinationals have relatively few activities, because it does not appear to be easy for them to transmit commercial operations through such countries, since all transactions must be domiciled at an authorized bank which is registered with the customs authority of the country concerned. How could British Leyland, for example, sell cars in Belgium after having put through the commercial operation fictitiously in the Bahamas with the consequent detriment to the Belgian Treasury and the British tax authorities?

Attempts to manipulate transfer prices can also be countered by internal restrictions created by the organization of the multinational itself. The manager of each subsidiary is judged by his financial results and it is therefore in his interest to maximize his profit and oppose excessive invoices. Such invoices would require frequent negotiations between the various branches of the company implicated in the transaction, as they would be obliged to adapt constantly to the evolution of foreign exchange rates and the fluctuations of the tax rates in the different countries.

The partial studies which exist on this question give, unfortunately, conflicting results. No indication of manipulation of transfer prices was detected for the multinationals in Canada's extraction industries,[37] but the reverse was true for multinationals dealing in pharmaceuticals in Colombia at the end of the sixties.[38]

With few statistics available, it is difficult to determine to what extent the trouble taken to manipulate prices proves worthwhile. Such practices imply a great risk of causing a scandal in exchange for relatively small gains. But a policeman lurking in the background does not necessarily frighten away a thief: he may simply use more imagination. Several well-publicized scandals are all we need for proof. Nevertheless, it is impossible to reject the reasoning of Robert Lattes when he says:

> If there is one thief in France, that doesn't mean that all Frenchmen are thieves and cannot in the least justify laws according to which we would all be potentially guilty.[39]

And what applies to France, is likely to be true elsewhere.

4 Multinationals and Society

To avoid any misunderstanding: the difference between American imperialism and Russian imperialism is the same as the difference between an old, satiated bandit whose reflexes are getting slower and slower, and a newly arrived, starving bandit who can only think about the looting to be done.

C. Castoriadis, *On War*, Paris:
Fayard (Coll. 'Les réalités'), 1981.

MULTINATIONALS AND POLITICS

This final chapter will discuss the relations of the multinationals to politics and then go on to their impact on social and cultural activities. The first part looks at the role of multinationals in the economic policy of the countries, in which they carry on their activities; the second part, with their intervention in national politics properly speaking and, in the third part, on the international political scene. In particular, the Codes of Conduct aimed at the multinationals will be examined.

ECONOMIC POLICY

In order to put the role of multinationals into perspective in relation to nations, we will successively look at what econ-

89

omic role is proper to a nation, its means of stimulation and control in relation to multinationals, and, lastly, the means at the disposal of the multinationals in their relations with nations. This does not necessarily imply a study of a conflicting relationship; rather, the power relations between two different actors, whose interests and actions are sometimes parallel, sometimes opposing.

The economic role of the nation

In discussing the economic role of a nation, it is necessary to distinguish between the action of the organizations it controls directly, that is government services and state-controlled firms and its influence on independent economic agents. Among national organizations, we usually make a distinction between government services like the National Health Service in Britain and state-controlled firms – such as BL and Rolls Royce Motors. This is a useful distinction in establishing the national budget and especially in defining the status of personnel. There can be civil servants with guaranteed employment, or employees on contract. The distinction varies from country to country.

  Another distinction is very useful in aiding the understanding of the economic reality of state-controlled organizations. On the one hand, state-controlled non-commercial organizations, like the Ministry of Education or the National Health Service, are financed by the government budget. On the other hand, state-controlled commercial organizations theoretically must survive on their own profit, whether they are in competition with private firms – like BL – or are monopolies like the National Coal Board.

  Because of the different governmental services it operates, and state-controlled firms, the government is most often the biggest employer in a country, but it is also the largest buyer of certain goods and services.

  The government has very powerful financial means. It indicates the rate of interest for the banks and controls the evolution of the money supply. These two arms of power have repercussions on the volume of investments of companies and on the rates of exchange. Some ministries can grant subsidies or funds for research which allow certain companies to develop activities in top priority sectors for the national economic policy. Moreover, the government can – and does – act as lender of last resort to industries in difficulty.

Table 4.1 gives a comparison of the number of employees in government services, state-controlled firms, local subsidiaries of foreign multinationals, and indigenous multinationals in Britain, France and the USA. The figures given should be viewed with caution, because they are the result of successive estimates.

It is interesting to note, however, that France with its emphasis on public services and centralized control has far fewer employees in government services (12.21 per cent) than either the United States or the United Kingdom (both over 20 per cent).

Government means

It is important to distinguish between the measures of the host countries and those of the multinationals' home countries. For the former, there are measures designed to stimulate or control foreign inward investments; for the latter, outward investments.

Most host countries which are the recipients of foreign investments have the power to investigate the activities of such companies within their territory. In fact, the host countries usually require that, in cases of acquisition or investments involving large sums of money, foreign investments are registered at an office in the Ministry of Finance. Some countries even require previous authorization of such investments. This is the case in France as well as in many countries in Mediterranean Europe and the developing countries, though not in other countries, including the United Kingdom. The various administrative conditions for the

TABLE 4.1 *Percentages of Total Employment Ascribable to Various Economic Agents (1976)*

Employment statistics 1976 Categories of economic agents	United Kingdom		France		United States	
	Number 000s	*% of total employment*	*Number 000s*	*% of total employment*	*Number 000s*	*% of total employment*
Government services [a]	5 300	21.37	2 546.5	12.21	18 060	20.64
State controlled firms	2 000	8.06	1 602.6	7.68	1 013	1.16
(including multinationals) [b]	360		820.3[f]			
Local subsidiaries of multinationals [c]	926	3.73	818	3.92	1 128.80	1.3
Private indigenous multinationals [d]	2 527	10.19	3 433	16[g]	11 830	13.52[h]
Other	14 047	56.64	12 455.90	60.20	55 453.20	63.38
Total employment [e]	24 800	100	20 856	100	87 485	100

SOURCES

a. : for UK, Social Trends, Table 4.7.
   : for France, figure given by the Direction Générale de l'Administration et de la fonction Publique.
   : for the United States, figure given by the Institut International d'Administration Publique.
b. : for UK, *The Times 1000*, 1977–78, Times Books.
   : for France, figure taken from 'L'Entreprise Publique dans la Communauté Economique Européenne', Centre Européen de l'Entreprise
     Publique, Brussels, 1981, p. 69.
   : for the United States, estimate made from information from various sources, among which the Union Postale Internationale and the
     Direction Générale des Télécommunications.

c. : for UK, a 1975 figure, John M. Stopford, *Employment Effects of Multinational Enterprises in the UK*, ILO Working paper, 5, Geneva, 1979.

  : for France, 1978 figure taken from 'L'implantation étrangère dans l'industrie au 1er janvier 1978', STISI, publication no. 18, p. 42.

  : for the United States, 1977 figure taken from Ned G. Howenstine, 'Selected Data on the Operations of US Affiliates of Foreign Companies', 1978 and 1979, in *Survey of Current Business* (May 1981), p. 40. The percentage in relation to national employment is calculated using total employment in 1977.

d. See Table 2.3 for UK, Social Trends, Table 4.7.

e. Labour Force Statistics, OECD, Department of Economics and Statistics, Paris, 1981, pp. 26–7.

f. Figure taken from Table 3.1 in this book.

g. Figure calculated by multiplying the value added due to the French subsidiaries of foreign multinationals (9.71 per cent: Table 2.1) by the ratio of the percentage of employees in the manufacturing industry due to indigenous multinationals and foreign multinationals ($40 : 19 = 2.1$; Table 2.3). We thus obtain 20.39 per cent of employment in France, or 4 253 000 persons, from which we subtract employment by the French state-controlled multinationals (820 300).

h. Figure obtained by taking the ratio of the number of persons employed by the American multinationals in the United States and that of those employed by the subsidiaries of foreign multinationals in the United States ($6\,700\,000 : 644\,000 = 10.4$; ILO, op. cit., p. 11) and multiplying that ratio by the percentage of employment in the United States due to the local subsidiaries of the multinational firms (1.3 per cent).

business activities of the local subsidiaries of foreign investors are very often strictly regulated. To begin with, they are regulated from a fiscal point of view. To encourage foreign investment, certain countries, especially developing countries, grant tax exemptions during the early years of activity of foreign companies. Limits may be set on the repatriation of dividends from the subsidiary to headquarters, again especially in developing countries. The same is true for the reimbursement of the interest on the loans granted by the home office to the subsidiary, as well as for the fees tied to management contracts and the royalties for patents. The governments of host countries may also impose a minimum percentage of locally-manufactured components in the finished product, as we saw in the case of the automobile industry. Government contracts can also be reserved for uninational firms. Thus, IBM lost the market for military electronics in France in the 1960s.[1]

Such stimulation and control has a short-term effect: local investment can increase and this is useful in a recession, because it creates jobs. A recent interesting example occurred in February 1982, when several members of the French Socialist Government, including the Prime Minister, made a special effort to explain the economic policy to foreign investors[2] to urge foreign multinationals to invest in France. On the contrary if a host country, particularly a developing one, is trying to protect its own infant industries for a time, so that they can develop their competence and productive capacity, before having to face foreign competition, it will look to the long-term effect. Using various means – customs duties, failure to deliver authorizations for investment – it will stop multinationals from setting up business.

The home countries most often require that they are informed of exports of capital when this is permissible in law. In certain countries – France, for example, unlike the United States or the United Kingdom – previous permission is necessary. Historically, exchange control in industrialized countries has discouraged direct investment in manufacturing abroad, though trade and servicing arrangements, which involve some foreign investments, have been encouraged where they were likely to aid exports. In developed countries, the export of capital is now generally permitted, especially to the extent that companies from these countries finance a large share of their expansion abroad by means of the capital market of the host countries, or the international money market. Examples of this at the end of the seventies were the very large German investments made in the United States and the purchase of Airco by British Oxygen and, at the end of 1981, the acquisition by the state-controlled French oil multinational Elf-Erap of the American firm Texas Gulf.

Research grants, loans at preferential rates for a specific project, equity participation, the creation of state-controlled firms, and preferential government contracts are measures which support home-based industrialists and reinforce their competitiveness. In the long run, too, this enables them to be in a better position in relation to their competitors when they decide to set up business abroad. The stimulation of investments abroad require greater financial means than those necessary for investments coming into a country from abroad. The results are also more difficult to achieve and can only be measured on a long-term basis with, however, one notable exception: export credit for industrial equipment sold with a transfer of technology.

The measures of control used by the governments of the host countries and the home countries of the multinationals vary a great deal from country to country. Control is at a minimum in countries with very powerful multinationals: the United States, West Germany, Great Britain, Holland and Switzerland. Stimulation by means of research grants and government contracts (including military purchases) exists on a large scale. Maximum control is used in the countries where multinationalization is average or low: France, Italy and, above all, the developing countries. The attitude of these countries has, however, been changing recently, as is the case in France. A developing country such as India also has a very favourable policy toward the multinationalization of its own companies, although there is very strict control on investments in India made by foreign companies.

The multinationals' means

The multinational companies have almost total freedom worldwide as far as their range of products is concerned, particularly for new products. In certain industries, however, like pharmaceuticals, for technical standards or consumer information, there are national standards. They are also, generally, totally free to develop new technologies in order to lower costs on existing products or create new products.

In their negotiations with different countries, the multinationals may create competition for the establishment of their factories. Such competition is based on the administrative conditions imposed by the national governments, which are not, however, necessarily enough to eliminate the advantages these countries present as far as the cost and quality of labour are concerned, or in the size of markets. On the other hand, it is obvious that the various countries can take advantage of the competition between the multinationals which themselves originate in different countries, or among several multinationals from the same country.

The multinationals can increase their autonomy in relation to the host countries by integrating production at the level of several countries (for example, through the EEC). In fact, each subsidiary becomes an integrated part of a plurinational system of production. Then, the nationalization of one of its parts, for example, would no longer make any sense. However, by lowering or eliminating these risks, a multinational becomes more vulnerable to an increase in customs duties, or to a strike at one production unit which could block production at all its European factories.

Centralization of Research and Development at the head office and the production of an uninterrupted flow of new technologies are also a way for multinationals to become indispensable to the different countries in which they carry on business. The link with the head office is essential to maintain the subsidiaries' capacity for innovation and for maintaining employment, which is very much in the interest of the host countries.

All this implies that multinational companies have a very large influence on the governments both of their home and their host countries. But, it is clear that the governments of these countries have the capacity to stimulate and control the multinationals to a very great extent. In general, an understanding between governments and companies can be reached because:

> Firms of whatever size are created with the purpose of producing and contributing to employment and development. They conform to the policies of the governments of the countries where they operate; in fact, they conform or they quit – *they* have to leave if there is disagreement or incompatibility.[3]

This is true whatever the size of the host country:

> I really do not see how the fact that the value of the world-wide sales of an international firm exceeds the national income of, say, Tanzania impairs in any way the ability of the government of Tanzania to reject its application to set up a subsidiary in the country, to restrict and regulate its activities if it is set up, or to expropriate an existing subsidiary.[4]

So, IBM and Coca Cola preferred to leave India rather than comply with the government requirements that local stockholders have a share of at least 51 per cent of the Indian subsidiaries of the two firms.

THE POLITICAL SCENE

Many people credit multinationals with the capacity to overthrow governments, influence or control the policies of certain countries, and corrupt the local civil servants and turn them into mere puppets advancing the interests of the multinational. Such views have their basis in several resounding scandals in the post-war period.

Political intervention

The most frequently cited example of the direct intervention of a multinational in a country is that of the American firm ITT which is alleged to have taken part in the overthrowing of the socialist government of President Allende in Chile at the beginning of the seventies. The US Senate hearings[5] revealed that Harold Geneen, President of ITT at the time, thought himself sent by God to fight against communism. He did, in fact, propose giving one million dollars to the CIA (the American secret service agency), to help it overthrow Allende. The CIA, however, refused. The Agency has a regularly allocated budget from the American government to finance its activities. As a matter of policy, it refuses private financing. Allende's Government was overthrown by that part of the Chilean military hierarchy which opposed him, very probably with the active aid of the CIA, but above all with the agreement of a large part of the local population: truck drivers, merchants, industrialists, and professionals, in particular, doctors.[6] ITT's action probably changed nothing in the sequence of events. Its lobbying was certainly not the sole factor in any orders which might have been given by the American Government to the CIA. On the other hand, the ensuing scandal had a devastating impact on the image of ITT for a brief period. Naturally the company became one of the favourite targets for the criticism levelled at multinationals in general.

When it comes to the increase in the price of petroleum, some observers are shocked by the pro-American policy followed by Saudi Arabia; for them, despite the nationalization of ARAMCO, the presence of American tankers is greater than ever and explains why Saudi Arabia is a 'puppet' of American foreign policy, a policy which itself was developed in the interest of the oil groups of the country. What is this all about?

When petroleum prices were increased beginning at the end of 1973, the American Government tried very hard to reduce the level of the increases as much as possible, because they increased the deficit in the American balance of payments. (The United States imports more than 50 per cent of its petroleum consumption.) Saudi Arabia has traditionally been the most moderate OPEC country when upward revisions in oil prices were discussed. The companies owning oil fields in the United States, however, should have been in favour of the higher prices: their exploitation costs remained stable while prices at which they sold were going up. Their profit soared and their interests thus paralleled those of the OPEC countries, which were asking for large price increases, and not those of the American Government.

On the other hand, it is interesting to see that the automobile manufacturers in the United States sought protection against Japanese car imports into their country. The action of these companies, together with that of the auto workers' union, reinforced the protectionism of the American Government. Negotiations with the Japanese Government led to 'voluntary' restrictions on the part of the Japanese exporters. As far as economic protectionism was concerned, there was unanimity. In this case, the uninational character of the activities of the parent company of these firms was much more important than their multinational character. This can be explained by the relative independence of the activities of the foreign factories of these groups and the activities of their parent company.

These three examples are good illustrations of the fact that the interests of the multinationals originating in a particular country are not always the same as the foreign or economic policies of that country. The multinationals' actions can reinforce those of the governments of their home countries, or weaken them, but they cannot mould policies all by themselves.

Bribes

Are bribes used by companies and governments for political ends? The existence of such practices has not been documented by serious, empirical studies. In fact, neither companies nor governments are willing to be interviewed about bribes. It is most likely, however, that they do exist, as certain scandals have indicated. These practices do not involve the multinationals in particular, but all economic agents. Corruption can very well exist among civil servants anywhere. Since electoral campaigns are costly and their sources of financing are not always made known to the public, it is likely that firms, both uninational and multinational, just like political parties or certain discretionary budgets of governmental agencies, feed these campaigns over and above anything which may be declared in their accounts. It would be in the interest of any company, moreover, to spread its finance among each of the competing camps in order to maintain good relations with everyone. As happened in the case of ITT in Chile, however, the executives of a company may commit themselves to one side because of their personal political preferences, rather than in the interest of the group they manage. They may of course believe sincerely that these are one and the same. It is not known to what extent these practices are commonplace; it is important, however, to emphasize the fact that in order to corrupt civil servants they must be willing. But certain countries and government agencies are well known for their dedication to public service, and anyone seeking to corrupt their civil servants risks imprisonment. Often scandals about bribes have concerned sales of arms abroad, involving sums frequently much larger than foreign investments normally made by companies.

The direct influence of the multinationals on the political scene properly speaking therefore seems to be rather limited. This is natural, since their domain is essentially economic. If their influence spreads to the political scene, it is because many observers confuse the political influence of the government of their home country with that of the companies originating in the same country. Of course, the two may generally agree, but this is not always the case. What is more, the political domain is often treated like an appendage of the economy – particularly by economists – since governments must protect the interests of their own companies. Such a mechanistic view of the relations between economics and politics was certainly incorrect at the beginning of the nineteenth century before the Industrial Revolution. It was surely much closer to reality from then until the middle of the twentieth century. Since then it is without a doubt erroneous. In a post-industrial society characterized by the importance of services and/or redistribution of income, the government plays a growing role. In developed countries, the most coveted social positions which include the greatest political and economic influence are achieved via a political role or a career in a large public organization, rather than through working in a private company. Indeed, a career in private industry in Britain tends to be scorned by the highly educated and qualified. The era of the great industrial empires is far away in the past. In the Eastern European countries and the developing countries, this trend is even clearer: to reach a position of power one must have had a military and political career rather than one in the economic domain. In post-industrial society, the hold of politics over the economy is much stronger than the reverse. But industrial society is still our recent past and so it is natural for its rationale to hide the realities of the functioning of the society in which we live today. The multinationals are the most advanced form of enterprise of the industrial era. Thus, they are automatically credited with a much greater influence in our society than they really have.

THE CODES OF CONDUCT

The first Code of Conduct for multinational companies was established by the International Chamber of Commerce in 1972.[7] It is not compulsory, and not only applies to the multinationals but also to the host and home countries of such companies. It is solely a question of recommendations for the governments of the countries and the companies involved. It suggests that the governments of the home countries should guarantee the operations of their companies against non-commercial, administrative and political risks; they should not insist on a minimum in the repatriation of dividends; the restrictions on capital export should be done away with; and, finally, corporate taxes on profits made abroad should take into account taxes paid in the host country and there should be no double taxation.

As for the host countries, the Code recommends that they adopt a policy of collaboration rather than of control *vis-à-vis* the multinationals; the participation of local shareholders should also be encouraged but not obligatory; there should be no restrictions on the repatriation of capital, on loans and dividends, or on royalties for technology.

For their part, the multinationals should inform the governments of their host countries of their plans, so that they can fit into the development objectives of those countries. They should try to choose local partners and offer them a share in the equity of their subsidiaries. They should volunteer information about their profits and be aware that sources of local financing may give priority to indigenous industrials. They should try to reinvest their profit locally, rather than repatriating it. They should also use local labour and give priority to local suppliers, above all in the developing countries.

This Code of Conduct was issued in response to the fears of the governments of the Third World countries about the actions of the representatives of the multinationals in their territories. It does not deal with the preoccupations of the trade unions.

This is not the case with OECD's Code of Conduct,[8] established in 1976. This Code was set up by the governments of the industrialized countries and has a great deal more influence than that of the International Chamber of Commerce, which left an opening for criticism for being too favourable to industry. Nevertheless, many Third World countries consider the OECD to be a 'club for the rich', since the headquarters of the largest multinationals are in countries which are members of the organization. The OECD Code, too, is a series of non-obligatory recommendations. It does not discriminate between multinational firms and uninational firms, but deals with the 'abnormal' activities of the former, the hypothesis being that their 'normal' activities have a positive effect. The Code is considered to be an obligation by those multinationals which mention in their annual report that they observe this Code.

The recommendations of the Code, the so-called 'guidelines', include six categories covering a great many of the activities of the companies: disclosure of information, competition, financing, taxation, science and technology, employment and industrial relations. Since the economic slowdown in 1974, the last category has taken on particular importance. Its principal elements are as follows: companies should recognize the trade unions and other employees' organizations; collective agreements should be signed with representatives of employees and information provided to them, so that they are able to negotiate effectively; the information should deal with the local subsidiary as well as with the multinational world-wide. The terms of employment for foreign workers should not be inferior to those in the parent company; the companies should use local labour; where a factory is closed down, the workers' representatives should be informed ahead of time and sufficient notice should be given; during negotiations, there should be no threats to transfer factories to another country; lastly, the union representatives should be able to negotiate with the representatives of the management who really make the relevant decisions.

These recommendations can be interpreted in two different ways. For instance, should the unions make claims which involve the risk of bankruptcy for the local subsidiary, the threat to transfer the factory then becomes legitimate. Although written in the form of recommendations, the

OECD Code has taken on an obligatory character through the Committee on International Investment and Multinational Enterprises (IME) which is made up of representatives of the governments of the OECD member countries. The unions cannot refer matters to the Committee directly – they must go through the representative of their country on the Committee. If the representative deems the case valid, he asks the opinion of the Committee in order to clarify the specific point in the Code of Conduct. As the opinion of the Committee is not necessarily followed by the government asking for it, the Committee is not seen as a court which judges the actions of the multinationals. However, thanks to the dynamism of the Trade Union Advisory Committee (TUAC) in its relations with the OECD, the opinions of the IME have had a favourable effect for the unions. The first case, discussed on 30 March 1977, was that of Badger, a Belgian subsidiary of Raytheon, the American multinational. Raytheon closed down the subsidiary, which was no longer profitable, making its 250 employees redundant. The unemployment compensation granted the employees in Belgium is among the highest in the world, and the local Raytheon management was reluctant to pay as it was bankrupt. The Government and the Belgian unions felt that the American parent should pay the compensation since it was responsible for the subsidiary. They deemed the behaviour of Raytheon contrary to the spirit of the OECD Code of Conduct and referred the case to the IME. Its interpretation was ambiguous, but nevertheless, shortly afterwards, the American multinational paid compensation which met with the satisfaction of the employees. It is reasonable to assume in this case that the OECD's Code of Conduct was used as a means of putting pressure on the multinational in question in order to bring it to make concessions to its employees.

Another Code, again in the form of non-obligatory recommendations, has been established since then. It was adopted in 1977 following a tripartite consultation between governments, representatives of employers and of workers meeting within the framework of the ILO, which gives it a great deal of importance. It deals solely with the social policy of the multinationals: employment, training, working conditions, living conditions, and professional relations.[9] Periodic reports on how it is working are made every two or three years by the governments of the signatory countries. A permanent tripartite commission was created in 1980 to examine the requests for interpretation of the declaration of principles. So far it has not had the opportunity to judge a case. The International Confederation of Free Trade Unions (ICFTU), which includes the main unions of the industrialized countries except for the Eastern European countries, adopted a charter for the multinational firms during its Congress in Mexico in October 1975.[10] The document requires the multinational firm to recognize its social responsibilities and recommends control of most operations in the host countries, or internationally.

Numerous Codes of Conduct for multinationals are being discussed at the United Nations and in its different agencies. The first was adopted by the United Nations Conference on Trade and Development (UNCTAD) in December 1980. It, too, is based on recommendations and is not obligatory. It deals with restrictive practices: cartel agreements on prices, collusion in take-over bids, the fixing of market shares, or sharing of clientele which could infringe the law of free competition. Any dominant position in a market should be examined in order to be sure that it does not hinder international competition.

A Code of Conduct was also adopted by the World Health Organization (WHO) in 1981 in relation to the trade practices in the sale of mother's milk substitutes in the developing countries. The text is the result of long preparation in conjunction with the United Nations International Children's Emergency Fund (UNICEF). The document stipulates primarily that the sale of all substitutes for mother's milk and other milk products should no longer be the object of any advertising, nor of any 'other form of promotion aimed at the general public'.[11]

Other Codes are still being negotiated, above all the

General Code of the United Nations, which is awaiting a consensus of member countries on the definition of multinational companies. The Eastern European countries do not want their foreign investments submitted to these Codes and some newly industrialized countries, particularly those in Latin America, also hope that only the activities of the multinationals from highly industrialized countries will be controlled.

The political process of elaboration of Codes of Conduct by international organizations was begun at the end of the 1960s when many people became aware of the considerable development of the multinational firms. It took some ten years to develop and began to bear fruit when the economic situation began to deteriorate. The general optimism of the 1960s gave way to the fears of the period of recession, felt very strongly in the mid-1970s and early 1980s. Under these circumstances, attitudes towards multinationals changed a great deal. The danger of 'loss of control' that they seemed to represent for governments and unions is becoming secondary to the contributions that they can bring to investment, technology and employment in the host countries. Added to that the resistance of the delegations from the industrialized countries in the international organizations which elaborate the Codes of Conduct, the unions as well as the representatives of the developing countries (the Group of 77) seem less active than before in requiring controls which might put into question the flow of international investments. Evidence of this can be seen with the diplomats representing Third World countries at these international negotiations. Their delegations are no longer led by ministers and ambassadors but by civil servants, indicating the lower priority now being given to these questions. The lack of unity among the countries of the Third World in this area is another explanation for the changing attitude. In fact, some newly industrialized countries like South Korea, Singapore and Formosa have a very rapid growth rate, which favours the development of their own multinationals. They can therefore, understand the reticence of the delegations from the highly industrialized countries. Moreover, certain Third World countries do not wish the Codes of Conduct to serve to augment union activity in their own countries, where unions are either outlawed or merely part of the government machinery. Lastly, they suspect the unions of the industrialized countries of wanting to use the Codes to protect employment in their own countries and diminish investment in the developing countries. Any demand for a detailed Code of Conduct administered by an international organization with all power to execute its judgements does not seem to be very realistic. The processes of negotiation and application of the Codes of Conduct, however, have allowed governments and unions to understand better the local and international actions of multinational companies and has given them the means to control them more effectively. The multinationals, although still able to carry out their own strategy, have lost a part of their freedom of initiative over the past twenty years.

THE MULTINATIONALS AND SOCIAL AND CULTURAL ACTIVITIES

MULTINATIONALS AND SOCIAL ACTIVITY

We will examine successively the impact of multinationals on work methods and habits, labour relations, and social change.

Impact on work methods

A very strong tendency toward uniformity in management methods in general developed in companies during the mid-sixties. The success of American companies at that time meant that their management methods became a model for companies and organizations of other countries. The European business schools quickly adopted the teaching methods of the North American business schools. But the model used was the success of American companies not of multinationals.

Within the multinationals themselves, the management methods of lower, middle and top executives are standardized. In fact, human resources management is coordinated at the international level to allow all the parts of the group to benefit from the talents discovered either in the subsidiaries or at head office. Before attaining positions in the general management, the executives must go abroad for periods varying from three to ten years to gain practical experience in management techniques in different countries. In this way, a particular identity develops in the executives of multinationals which, although it takes into account the different conditions prevailing in each country, means that all the executives can communicate with one another and avoid cultural misunderstandings. This common identity in the technical, commercial and financial domains is the result of the immersion of every executive working in the companies with their methods and habits which have been progressively built up throughout their history.

Such a culture is highly influenced by the country of origin of the multinational. For example, in their system of incentives and rewards, the Americans usually include the possibility of the participation in profit-sharing for their executives. This is done through stock options sold at a lower price than that on the market. This is one North American habit that has not spread to many European multinationals.

The internationalization of work methods and their standardization within the same multinational have been developed much less for employees and workers than for executives. For example, in contrast to the Europeans, American workers still have short vacations. The French workers of American and Swiss multinationals have five weeks of paid holiday, whereas those of their parent companies have an average of two and four respectively. Salaries also vary according to the country in which the subsidiaries of the multinationals carry on their activities. In fact, wages in each country are a result of negotiations between the local unions and employers. In particular, the workers in the subsidiaries in the developing countries have salaries which are comparable to the salaries of the workers in local companies and not those in the subsidiaries in the developed countries. This is because among local employers the weight of the uninational companies and the indigenous multinationals is much greater than that of the local subsidiaries of the foreign multinationals, as was seen in the previous chapter.

However, the multinationals, in order to be sure to have high-quality, dependable personnel, often pay salaries which are slightly higher than those of the local firms. The general increase in purchasing power for employees cannot, however, be attributed to the multinationals. It is due to the increase in the general productivity of labour and, in a more general way, to economic growth. This growth permitted the employees' organizations to help their members benefit from its fruits until the mid-seventies.

In the developing countries, where economic activity was largely based on agriculture and handcrafts before the First World War, the birth of the industrial age brought rapid and brutal transformations of industrial relations. The introduction of fixed working hours and an obligatory number of working days led to strong resistance, with higher rates of absenteeism than in countries already industrialized. In some countries, the firms organize transport to the place of work for their workers. The rapidity of social change is only due in part to the actions of the multinationals. In fact, local companies – whether private or state-controlled – have used modern industrial practices by applying the models of developed countries. As multinationals represent only a very small percentage of local employment, it would seem difficult to hold them alone responsible for the break with the previous methods of production. It is rather a case of the general behaviour of all firms favourable to 'modernistic' solutions.

Relations with the labour unions

The multinationalization of firms has not been paralleled by an equally large multinationalization of the trade unions. Unions are still organized on an essentially national basis and, within this framework, the differences are very great. Certain countries like the United Kingdom, West Germany and Belgium have very powerful unions, centered primarily on the promotion and defence of the interests of their members. They are securely implanted in companies and the rate of unionization is high. In the United States, too, though the degree of unionization is lower, the unions which do exist are extremely powerful. In countries like France or Italy, in contrast, the unions are much more divided and the divergent views of the political parties in these countries are also present within the union movement. The rate of unionization is much lower and their influence weaker. In the developing countries, the unions are not very well represented, partly because freedom to organize may not be permitted. Any collaboration between these very different types of union on a world-wide basis is therefore highly delicate. No one union federation can impose its will on others located in different countries.

Nevertheless, the unions of the European countries are grouped together within the European Confederation of Trade Unions (ECTU). They exchange information to promote their interests in member countries and their activities mainly cover the problem which they all face of the Codes of Conduct destined for multinationals. A charter for the multinationals has been developed by the International Confederation of Free Trade Unions (ICFTU) of which the main unions of the Anglo-Saxon countries are members. They have no common activities with the World Labour Federation which represents the denominational unions, or the World Federation of Trade Unions (WFTU), made up of the unions of the Eastern European countries.

When it comes to specific actions in the defence of employees, two types of behaviour have appeared on the

scene. The first is that the workers in a factory located in one
country manifest their solidarity with those in the factories
belonging to the same multinational in neighbouring countries by refusing to do overtime. As a result, the international
management of the group cannot compensate for a lack of
production in one country by increasing production in the
factories of the neighbouring countries. The second is for
workers of the different factories of a multinational to go on
strike at the same time as a means of showing their opposition
to the international restructuring of production which would
lead to lay-offs in the sister subsidiaries. This happened, for
example, in the factories of the Dutch chemical multinational,
AKZO. Although such defensive actions have taken place,
collective negotiations throughout the groups to determine
general levels of salaries and working conditions have not
been successful, because of the very large differences between the countries in which a multinational operates.

Moreover, since the economic changes which occurred in
the mid-seventies, union activity is no longer directed to
getting the benefits of growth for its members, but of
safeguarding jobs in the industrial sector. The number of
employees in this sector is after all diminishing. In the case of
the automobile industry, for example, it would be difficult for
American and Japanese workers to undertake common
action when what we are seeing is agreements between
American workers, industrialists and government on a
protectionist basis.[12] It is not the first time in history that
nationalism takes precedence over internationalism in times
of recession.

Multinationals and social change

The labour movement was the primary social movement in
the nineteenth century and the first half of the twentieth
century and it was organized essentially on a national basis. It
had its own identity and opposed the conduct of politicians
and industrialists who were setting to work the principles of a

competitive economy based on free, private enterprise. The trade unions and the workers' parties sought control over all aspects of society without, however, wanting to change its direction. In fact, all the actors on the political scene agreed to work towards human progress through science, technology, and industrialization.

Since the trade union movement was diluted into laws, institutions and political parties which gave recognition to a great many of its claims, there has been no new social movement of the same importance to replace it. The social movement based on anti-nuclear and ecological sentiments,[13] for example, has not taken its place as a principal element in the understanding of the production of society. Indeed, the very notion of social movement has perhaps been put in question.

The bases of the trade union movement and the anti-nuclear movement are essentially national; these movements were and are very different in Britain, the United States and Germany, for example. It is enough to observe that the multinationals were not the driving force of the fight against the trade union movement, because they were at their very beginnings when the labour movement was at its apogee. As for defining the priorities of nuclear power following the increase in the price of petroleum, this was done by the governments of the different countries, often influenced by state-controlled national firms such as the Central Electricity Generating Board or, to a lesser extent, the United Kingdom Atomic Energy Authority. The multinationals played a minor role.[14] They are accelerators of development in the developed and developing countries and participate in social change, sometimes activating it. They are not the principal determining factor, nor are they masters of the directions in which they move. It is the society of which the executives of multinationals are a part, like the leaders of all the large, complex organizations, be they economic, political, or governmental, uninational or international, which determines these orientations.

MULTINATIONALS AND CULTURAL ACTIVITY

We often hear that multinationals export the culture of their home country. In the industrialized countries it is said that American companies impose their culture on Europe and Japan; in the developing countries, that the multinationals of the industrialized countries impose a way of life and a Western culture synonymous with a brutal social break and the negation of the identity of the host countries. Two examples, illustrate their views.

Culture and identity

The critics of the multinationals offer the same explanation for the spread of the culture of the industrialized countries as they do for the introduction of production techniques. American companies develop cultural products to suit American markets and then export them to Europe and Japan by means of their local subsidiaries.

Pop music is an example. With a few exceptions (salsa, reggae) this type of music originates in the United States: jazz, rock, disco, and so on. Its success in America spread almost immediately to the European countries. One might consider that this was a process of cultural propagation imposed by the head offices of American multinationals on their subsidiaries and the European consumers, in other words, a sign of the cultural domination of Europe by the United States. A recent empirical study[15] upsets this view. In fact, the British or French subsidiaries of American multinationals do not market the biggest American hits in these two countries. It is uninational European companies with no financial ties with America which sell the records. They buy the marketing rights. American companies, because of the extent of their financial resources, could very easily acquire these European competitors or else try to create a 'brain drain' of their artistic managers, who know how to spot a potential hit. But they do not do this. We are therefore confronted much more with a reappropriation by the local companies of a foreign culture than by the spreading of a dominant culture. There are many areas where tastes converge from one country to another and certain singers can be successful in several countries at the same time.

As for models of food consumption, the American firms developed frozen foods in their country during the sixties. In Europe, the development of the sale of frozen foods did not take place before the seventies. Again, this was done not by the American multinationals but by European companies. The Findus brand is particularly successful and, according to the country, belongs either to Unilever or Nestlé, both food industry multinationals of European origin (Anglo-Dutch and Swiss respectively). It is interesting moreover, to note that the two largest multinationals in the food industry worldwide are these two European companies.

In the field of fast foods, the first to set up business for the sale of hamburgers and Coca-Cola on the European continent were the local subsidiaries of Wimpy, a British multinational. In France, the wide success of McDonald's – America's top hamburger specialist – has its own unique history. A Frenchman of Moroccan origin was so successful at setting up hamburger 'joints' in Chicago that the management of McDonalds in the USA, who wanted to manage those joints directly, gave him the exclusive right to open McDonalds restaurants in France, as a compensation for giving up the Chicago business. At the time, the Americans did not believe their methods could work in France. In 1982, however, they took their former collaborator to court to try to stop him from using the name McDonalds. The judgment was favourable to McDonalds who recovered it for their own development projects in France. Their former manager labelled his joints O'Kitch.

We can observe, therefore, a certain standardization of cultures in the industrialized countries. This standardization is essentially due to similar patterns of consumption and taste, often influenced by the American example. The multinationals may be the vehicles for this standardization – and that would be the propagation of the cultural model. Local firms may also be the vehicle, and that is the reappropriation of a foreign culture by imitation and adaptation. It is therefore important to make the distinction between the nature of the culture transmitted and the national origins of the supplier: the two do not necessarily correspond. This could easily be illustrated by other examples from the cinema and education, communications, health and education.

However, the tendency toward the cultural standardization of the industrialized countries does not mean that each of them cannot safeguard its identity. Each has a different history. The same period of history can even be interpreted in the completely opposite way on two sides of the same political frontier. Thus, the teaching of the Napoleonic period is not the same in France as in the neighbouring countries where Napoleon's army wreaked havoc, or in Britain which defeated Napoleon. Cultural particularities other than language, which is difficult to standardize, resist normalization. The national systems of education, health, and social welfare are specific to each country, even in Europe. They are not changed by looking at the example of neighbouring countries but by negotiations on a national basis between the trade unions and the government. Moreover, there is even a resurgence of regional cultures since the 1970s: plays in Provençal or Breton in France, and the growth of Welsh and Scottish nationalism in Britain are examples.

Developing countries: dependence or development?

The question of the role of the multinationals in the culture and the identity of the developing countries is different from that in the industrialized countries. We no longer need to know if the multinationals are responsible for, or participate in, the standardization of cultures, but rather if they have a part in the economic, social and cultural development of these countries or if, on the contrary, they impose an industrialized culture reserved for a small part of the population, casting the overwhelming majority into misery and famine, aggravating underdevelopment and shattering the identity of the countries by rendering them totally dependent. Three different answers to this question have been elaborated.

The first is the theory of the 'stages of economic growth' which appeared at the end of the Second World War. It assumed that the stages of industrialization in the developing countries would automatically follow the same pattern as that experienced by the developed countries.[16] The five stages in the growth of an industrial society are: traditional society; preconditions for take-off into industry, which depend upon the development of education, a centralized state, and some technological development; the take-off itself, during which the forces towards economic progress dominate not only investment and technology but also political groups; the drive to maturity, during which industries more sophisticated than the basic primary sectors develop; and, finally, the age of high mass-consumption and the diffusion of services on a mass scale, based not only on new technologies but also on the redistribution of income and the development of a social welfare system.

The hypothesis behind the theory of the 'stages of economic growth' is that the development of the non-industrialized countries would take place in a way analogous to that of the industrialized countries. This hypothesis does not hold up against the reality of the hold which the industrialized countries have had over the developing countries, during the colonial or the post-colonial periods. This is the point of departure for the theory of 'dependence', developed during the 1940s by Latin American theoreticians[17] and taken up again twenty years later by French-speaking Marxist theorists.[18] The theory of dependence has economic implications: it suggests that the industrialization of the countries of the South cannot take place autonomously and simply for the local market; on the contrary, it must be developed through the export of agricultural and industrial raw materials to the North, in exchange for industrial goods. The terms of trade are so unfavourable to the countries in the South that they cannot go about their own development independently. The social implication is that these countries are split into a dual society, between the half which works for the export sector and the other half, which not only does not benefit from growth, but is also thrown into a situation worse than the one existing before. Even so, this latter half becomes part of the modern world because of its economic demands; but those involved do not have the means to satisfy their demands, because the fruits of their labour are not marketed or, if they are, only in terms of increasing poverty. In matters of culture, dependence implies the end to the former national identity without it being replaced by a new national identity.

So what is happening is increasing underdevelopment,[19] with more than half of the population set aside from social progress. According to Gunder Frank, the only solution is socialist revolution. Another version of the theory of dependence is based on the transfer of capital gains from the developing countries to the developed countries.[20]

Dual society or the wrong type of development[21] implies that the developing countries are entirely dependent on the countries in the North and so cannot move through the various stages of industrial growth as did the latter, or reach autonomous development, which would permit them to break the vicious circle of the dual society and allow the whole population to participate in the process of development. Economic growth is therefore not synonymous with economic social and cultural development.

These theories, essentially economic theories, have been criticized, in particular by certain sociologists.[22] For them, history does not produce men: men – particularly social classes – produce their own history. As a result, what will happen cannot be determined ahead of time by an all-powerful god or an 'iron law' of capitalism. They claim that the extension of the development of the nations of the South to all the categories of the population will depend on the power relationships between the different social forces of these countries, including those dealing with foreign capital.

Do multinationals play any role in this process of dependence or development? The theories mentioned above give them little importance because they are mainly based on exchange, that is, international trade, whereas the activities of multinationals properly speaking, are based principally on production for local markets. Nevertheless, it is interesting to note that the breach in the traditional way of life is attributed to the multinationals because of the cultural bias they bring. It is often claimed that they brutally impose a Western-style culture on rich as well as poor consumers and so destroy the old way of life and the national identity of these countries. But the very concept of culture implies cultivating, educating with vitality and creative force, as much as identifying a pattern of behaviour in a country. In fact, most developing countries have a past dominated by colonialism dating from well before the establishment of the multinationals. They were in contact with a foreign culture, English, French, or Spanish, for example, through colonial administrations. These administrations set up systems of education and health, an army and a police force which were taken over by the new leaders of the countries when they became independent. This cultural infrastructure certainly had a much deeper, much more durable impact on former colonies than any finished goods which came in exchange for exported raw materials. Since independence, the multinationals, through the increase in exports and imports which they imply and through their local production, have certainly accelerated the replacement of an old way of life by a new one. But, just as in the industrialized countries, they do so within a framework and in a certain direction; in both cases they participate without being the sole force determining events.

An interesting exercise[23] consists in setting the reality of the multinationals against the idea of what endogenous development of the developing countries might otherwise be. The exercise seeks to discover what the governments of these countries could do to ensure national control of communications, education, science and technology in a way which would allow them to develop an alternative civilization, less industrialized and more human. All the suggestions made can be compared with the practices of the governments of the countries. The two are totally divorced. To attribute the responsibility for all the cultural developments in society to the economic reality of the multinationals, is once again to take the cultural, social and political domains as a direct function of the economy. This conception of society has no explanation for the behaviour of the governments of the developing countries. As explained above, they are not the puppets of the multinationals, but they do share with the multinationals the idea that progress in society is synonymous with the progress of science and technology, which leads to an increase in industrial output.

It is obvious that multinationals are interested in profitable production and sales and that they deal with a rich clientele to the exclusion of those whose purchasing power is insufficient to allow them to consume industrial goods. The same is true of the uninational firms of these countries which compete with the local establishments of the multinationals. That is not an imposed cultural model; it is the appropriation by the local producers and consumers of a cultural model which suits them. The effects are not always those which are expected and can, in some cases, rebound against the companies. An example is the way that the ownership of television sets increases absenteeism in factories a great deal during World Cup soccer games. Failure to turn up for work cannot possibly have been the aim of these companies selling television sets.

Beside the propagation of an industrial culture for a part of the population, an older cultural identity is very strongly maintained, just as in the developed countries.

Conclusion

In Chapter 1, we saw that early development of the multinationals, which dates from the end of the nineteenth century, was not sustained. It was interrupted by the Russian Revolution and also by the two World Wars; later, it underwent profound transformations following the change in the world's economy, as a result of the sharp rise in the prices of petroleum. The spread of multinationals, which was an essentially North American phenomenon after the Second World War, has become a world-wide phenomenon since the end of the sixties, originating primarily in the industrialized countries which are not only their home countries but also the countries in which they mostly invest.

The multinationals were first established in the primary sector for extraction of raw materials, but were forced out of mining when the developing countries decided to take control of the resources in their subsoil. The multinationals nevertheless maintain an essential downstream role in the refining and marketing of the derivatives of raw materials. In manufacturing, American multinationals' ascendency is giving way to the growing European and Japanese multinationals. In the economic history of the twentieth century, the major strategic decisions of the multinationals were made partially on their own initiative and partially in compliance with government decisions: variation in customs duties, obligations to use components manufactured locally, and diverse manufacturing and other regulations. In the service industries, the multinationals, especially the banking multinationals, developed their activities abroad in order to follow the manufacturing clients of their home countries.

Chapter 2 examined how multinationals function internally and in the market-place. Internal practice is guided mainly by the goal of survival, which varies according to the country in which the activity is taking place. Their organization is complex, as it must take into account regional differences and product diversification. Decisions are the product of a long, interactive, internal process, the results of which are largely influenced by forces inside and outside of the multinationals.

When it comes to their external operations, we saw that the local subsidiaries of the foreign multinational companies represent approximately 20 per cent of the value added of the manufacturing industry of the host countries, or 5 to 10 per cent of gross national product. Nevertheless, the activity of an indigenous multinational is twice as important in its home country as that of foreign multinationals there. Further, the growth of multinationals is not a result of the concentration of a small number of companies, but of an increase in the number of multinationals in the industrial sector. Despite their development in the services industries, they have not deeply penetrated that sector, which by its very nature lends itself less to multinationalization. It would seem difficult, therefore, for the multinationals to assume increasing control over the economies of post-industrial society.

Chapter 3 established the fact that the indigenous and foreign multinationals are responsible for 10–15 per cent of employment in industrialized countries and only 2 per cent in developing countries. Employment due to the indigenous multinationals in their home countries is, on the average, twice as large as that due to the foreign multinationals. Globally speaking, employment created by the multinationals is slightly less important than that created by governments. It is concentrated in manufacturing with 40–60 per cent taken by the multinationals – figures for the indigenous multinationals are once again twice the level of those for the foreign multinationals. They increase employment in their foreign subsidiaries more than in their home countries, but since the world recession they do not seem to be shedding labour at a greater rate than other companies in the host countries.

As far as speculation in foreign currencies is concerned, multinationals do not seem to play an essential role. It is the banks, through their activities on the foreign exchange market, and influenced by the different rates of interest (and inflation) in differing countries, which produce changes in rates of exchange.

Multinationals, however, are no doubt a factor in the acceleration of development in industrialized countries and in the economic growth of developing countries because of the technology they transfer internally to their foreign subsidiaries, or externally to local firms.

Chapter 4 showed that the multinationals' role in economic policy in the host and home countries is an important but not dominant one. In fact, the governments of these countries have very great powers which give them the last word in cases of conflict with the multinationals, through their central administrations and state-controlled companies, as well as through the stimulation and controls that they exercise in the economies of their countries, which apply as much to uninational firms as to indigenous and foreign multinationals. The latter are not directly able to overthrow governments either – that is the result of a political process internal to each country. If any foreign intervention takes place, it is on the part of foreign governments not companies. The actions of the foreign multinationals in those countries may parallel or conflict with the actions of their governments, as several examples have shown.

The development of Codes of Conduct has been an element used, in particular by the trade unions, to lead certain multinationals to grant more favourable conditions to their employees and to the governments of the host countries. However, the protectionism which has developed since the adjustment process in the mid-seventies to safeguard employment seems to hamper the creation of obligatory codes governed by international organizations.

The multinationals, accelerators of social and cultural change, are one of many factors taking part in these changes. In fact, the local companies of the host countries appropriate

– often as quickly or better than the multinationals – the products or social practices developed by the latter. The executives of the multinationals are like anyone else, part of society. They play an essential role, but they do not necessarily determine the direction in which society is headed. That is much more the affair of the political bodies which make decisions deemed legitimate by all the citizens. In the developing countries, multinationals contribute to industrial growth and participate in the transformation of local culture. Nevertheless, this process had begun during the period of colonization and was reappropriated to a very large extent by local governments and companies, which represent the essential part of economic, social and cultural activity in these nations.

It is now easier to separate myth from reality as far as the multinationals are concerned. They are definitely active and powerful, especially in their home countries and in the industrial sector. But they are not necessarily the most powerful of the mighty. Moreover, their future is largely linked to an economic sector which is declining, relatively speaking: manufacturing industry. In fact, service industries and the redistribution of income play a preponderant role in post-industrial societies.

Multinationals are secretive just like any large, complex organization. Companies, governments, political parties and trade unions, all act with their objectives in mind and not for the purpose of explaining their behaviour to the outside world. Researchers in the social sciences have, therefore, a broad field to examine in order to understand the operation and impact of the multinationals as well as that of all complex organizations. Their action is beneficial for the readers who favour consumer societies where social progress through technological innovation is implicit in the political ideology. Their opinion will concur with that of most of the leaders of all the large, complex organizations whose orientation is the same as that of the multinationals. The reader who finds their action nefarious will similarly oppose the direction given to society by the complex economic, political and trade union organizations. Unless he seeks another type of society, he will no doubt prefer a balance between the different existing forces. For that to happen, limits to the unilateral action by all large organizations are necessary, including that of multinationals. If it were done solely for the multinationals, would there not be a risk of creating new imbalances and new monsters?

Notes and References

INTRODUCTION

1. J. Attali, M. Holthus, D. Kebschull, G. Peninou, P. Uri, *Who's afraid of multinationals?* (Brussels: ECSIM; London: Saxon House, 1978).
2. Ibid., p. 30.
3. In general, definitions vary from one to six subsidiaries and from 5–50 per cent of the turnover. The choice here is made to avoid a long discussion.
4. J. Savary, *The French Multinationals* (Paris: PUF–IRM, 1981), p. 44.
5. For example: 'large national firm possessing or controlling several production subsidiaries in several countries.' C. A. Michelet, *Le Capitalisme mondial* (World Capitalism) (Paris: PUF, 1976), p. 20.
6. There is still no true definition of the transnational firm, but in general the United Nations refers to a series of characteristics listed in G. Schetting, 'On the Definition of Transnational Corporations in a UN Code of Conduct', *Intereconomics* (March/April 1980), p. 76.
7. B. Madeuf, *L'ordre technologique international* (The International Technological Order) (Paris: La Documentation Française, 1981).
8. When Anglo-Dutch Unilever and Nestlé of Switzerland were involved in a joint company in the German frozen food industry (Unilever had the majority holding), they were each making an external transfer. When Unilever opens a frozen food factory of its own in an African country, it is making an internal transfer of technology.
9. The term uninational was first used in France by Dr Michel Ghertman and has now become generally accepted.

CHAPTER 1: HOW MULTINATIONALS DEVELOPED

1. 1902: from a speech by William Lever.
2. BOC's move into North America occurred in the early 1970s, apparently as an answer to L'Air Liquide's entry into the USA a few years earlier. It was not an on-the-spot reaction to US competition in the UK, because American firms came to Britain in the early 1960s.
3. Popularized by J. J. Servan-Schreiber's book *Le défi américain* (The American Challenge) (Paris: Denoel, 1967).
4. R. Vernon, 'International Investment and International Trade in the Product Cycle', *Quarterly Journal of Economics*, vol. LXXX, no. 2

(May 1966): pp. 191–207. See M. Rainelli, *La Multinationalisation des firmes* (The Multinationalization of Firms) (Paris: Economica, 1979) for more extensive information and a summary of existing theories.

5. Created by the Treaty of Rome on 25 March 1957. Association of the principal European countries for standardization of customs tariffs and a common agricultural policy.

6. Thus in 1950, 38 per cent of American investments were concentrated in Latin America. In 1970 they had fallen to 15 per cent. During the same years their investments in Europe and Canada went from 45 per cent to 60 per cent of their total foreign investments. (J. Wilkie, *Statistics and National Policy* (Los Angeles: UCLA Latin American Center, 1974): Annex B.)

7. Bank for International Settlements, Basel, 46th and 51st Reports; and OECD, *Main Economic Indicators*, 1960–79 and 1982.

8. J. Pelkmans, *Intereconomics*, HWWA, vol. 17, no. 2 (March–April 1982), Table 3, p. 58.

9. E. Zaleski and H. Wienert, *Technology Transfer Between East and West* (Paris: OECD, 1980); and M. T. Skully, *A Multinational Look at the Transnational Corporation* (Sydney, Australia: Dreyden Press), pp. 259 *et seq.*

10. B. Lietaer, *Le Grand Jeu Europe/Amérique Latine* (Europe and Latin America and the Multinationals) (Paris: PUF–IRM, 1982), pp. 132 *et seq.*

11. A. Sampson, *The Seven Sisters: the Great Oil Companies and the World They Made* (London, Sydney, Auckland: Hodder and Stoughton, 1975).

12. E. L. Dalemont, *L'Industrie du pétrole* (Paris: PUF, 1980), pp. 20–1.

13. When oil was found in the North Sea, the British National Oil Company was formed in the late 1960s by the then Labour administration. This company is a state corporation owning the oil resources, which then licenced the fields to the various operating companies. The Conservative Thatcher administration plans to 'privatise' BNOC and sell it off to private investors.

14. E. L. Dalemont, *L'Industrie du pétrole* (Paris: PUF, 1980).

15. Formerly Standard Oil. The name was changed when the company celebrated 80 years of existence. Exxon's European name is Esso.

16. 1981 sales figures for these companies in millions of sterling. In parentheses is their rank among the world's largest firms: Exxon (1): 65 039.9; Royal Dutch/Shell (2): 46 956.0; Mobil (3): 38 849.2; Texaco (5): 38 110.0; British Petroleum (6): 30 624.0; Standard Oil of California (7): 25 986.2; Gulf Oil (10): 17 250.8; Compagnie Française des Pétroles (15): 10 389.6. Source: *The Times* 1000, 1982–83.

17. Sid Ahmed, *L'OPEP, passé, présent et perspectives* (OPEC–Past, Present and Perspectives) (Paris: Economica, 1980), pp. 6 *et seq.* and 141; and République algérienne démocratique populaire, *Le pétrole, les matières premières de base et le développement* (Petroleum, Basic Raw Materials, and Development). Report presented by Algeria at the extraordinary session of the United Nations General Assembly (Algiers: Sonatrach, 1974), pp. 135 *et seq.*

18. The Russian firm, Nafta UK has a one per cent share of Britain's oil distribution.
19. E. L. Dalemont, *L'industrie du Pétrole* (Petroleum) (Paris: PUF, 1980).
20. Within these groups, however, there is a big difference between those which own oil fields in the USA (Exxon and Royal Dutch/Shell) and those which do not (CFP). The first two are much more profitable than the CFP, since they supply their refineries with much cheaper crude. The French multinational, whose supply of crude comes from OPEC countries, must pay the price on the international market.
21. G. Chandler, 'The Innocence of Oil Companies', *Foreign Policy*, vol. 27 (Summer 1977), p. 60.
22. *Transnational Corporations in the Copper Industry* (New York: United Nations, 1981).
23. *Transnational Corporations in World Development: a Re-Examination* (New York: United Nations, 20 March 1978), p. 234.
24. J. M. Stopford, J. H. Dunning, K. O. Haberich, *The World Directory of Multinational Enterprise* (London: Macmillan Press, 1980), p. 301.
25. G. Maxcy, *The Multinational Motor Industry* (London: Croom Helm, 1981), p. 63.
26. Ibid., p. 69.
27. M. Wilkins and F. E. Hill, *American Business Abroad: Ford on Six Continents* (Detroit: Wayne State University Press, 1964), pp. 247 *et seq.*
28. G. Maxcy, op. cit., p. 87.
29. Ibid., p. 108.
30. Ibid., p. 163.
31. Ibid., p. 163.
32. *Transnational Banks: Operations, Strategies and Their Effects in Developing Countries* (New York: United Nations, 1981), pp. 40, 41.
33. Ibid., pp. 124–6.
34. Ibid., pp. 26–7.
35. Ibid., p. 28.
36. Wrongly called 'crisis'. See A. Touraine, *'Crise ou mutation?'*, *Au-delà de la crise* ('Crisis or Adjustment Process?' Beyond the Crisis) (Paris: Le Seuil, 1976), pp. 23–55.

CHAPTER 2: HOW MULTINATIONALS FUNCTION

1. Examples: –small or medium-sized British multinationals: Booker McConnell, Consolidated Gold Fields, Brooke Bond Group.
   –large enterprises (fewer than 100 000 employees): Rio Tinto Zinc (UK), Lafarge (French mining and industrial cement factories), SA Cockerill (Belgian steel-works), Atlas Copco AB (Swedish pneumatic tools), Suzuki Motor Company Limited (Japanese motorcycles), Kodak (US photographic).

–giants (more than 100 000 employees): Exxon (American oil company whose products are marketed in Britain under the trade name of Esso), Renault (French automobile manufacturers), IBM (American electronics), Royal Dutch/Shell (Anglo-Dutch company whose products are marketed under the name Shell), Siemens (German electrical equipment), BAT Industries (UK tobacco, retailing, printing and packaging), British Petroleum, Dunlop (UK rubber goods).

–well-known companies: Sony (Japanese electronics), Barclays Bank, Coca Cola, Polaroid.

2. M. Ghertman, *La Prise de décision* (The Making of Decisions) (Paris: PUF–IRM, 1981).
3. Morgan International Data, December 1982, Table 2.
4. E. Malinvaud, *Initiation à la comptabilité nationale* (Initiation to National Accounting) (Paris: INSEE, 1973).
5. John Cantwell, Reading University.
6. J. Savary, op. cit., pp. 35–8, showed this for French firms. The assumption is not yet verified by empirical research for other countries.
7. CNRS, *La croissance de la grande firme multinationale* (The Growth of the Large Multinational Firm) (Paris: Editions du CNRS, 1973).
8. *Transnational Corporations in World Development: A Re-examination*, New York, United Nations, 20 March 1978.
9. Ibid.
10. ILO, op. cit., p. 95.
11. F. Fishwick, *Multinational Companies and Economic Concentration in Europe* (London: Gower, 1982), p. 82.
12. Ibid. p. 77.
13. Ibid. p. 78.
14. G. Modelski, *Transnational Corporations and World Order* (San Francisco: W. H. Freeman, 1979), pp. 45–65.
15. Ibid. p. 51.
16. *Directory of the World's Largest Firms* (London: Macmillan, 1983), vol. 3.
17. J. H. Dunning and R. Pierce, *World's Largest Industrial Enterprises* (London: Gower, 1981). A sample of 482 firms.
18. Ibid.
19. R. Vernon, *Sovereignty at Bay* (London: Longman, 1971).
20. Fishwick, *Multinational Companies and Economic Concentration in Europe* (London: Gower, 1982).
21. Ibid.

CHAPTER 3: THE ROLE OF THE MULTINATIONALS IN THE ECONOMY

1. Yearbook of Labour Statistics (Geneva: ILO, 1981); excepting the Eastern European countries (Comecon), China, Cuba, etc.: estimates from IRM documentation.

2. ILO, op. cit., p. 3.
3. See Table 4.1 in Chapter 4 (United Kingdom and the United States only: 5 300 000 and 18 060 000 respectively).
4. Member countries of the OECD are Canada, United States, Japan, Australia, New Zealand, Austria, Belgium, Denmark, Spain, Finland, France, Greece, Iceland, Ireland, Italy, Luxembourg, Norway, the Netherlands, Portugal, Germany, the United Kingdom, Sweden, Switzerland and Turkey.
5. ILO and IRM. John Cantwell, Reading University.
6. This average covers very great differences: from only 2 per cent in Japan to 43 per cent for Canada.
7. Ibid.
8. Using the figures for total world employment (1 568 million in 1980, including 992 million in the developing countries and 576 million in the developed countries – see Y. Sabolo, 'Emploi et chomage, 1960–1990' (Employment and Unemployment, 1960–1990. *International Labour Review*, vol. 112, no. 6, December 1975), the percentage of the employment due to the multinationals would seem to be less than one-third of that calculated using the figures for salaried workers only.
9. M. Ghertman, *Les Multinationales* (PUF, Paris 1982), p. 63.
10. ILO, op. cit., p. 95.
11. Savary, op. cit., p. 111.
12. Savary, ibid., p. 171.
13. Savary, ibid., pp. 154–65.
14. D. Van den Bulcke and E. Halsberghe, 'Employment Effects of Multinational Enterprises: Belgian Case Study', ILO, Working Paper no. 1, 1979, pp. 50–1.
15. A. Touraine, *La Société post-industrielle* (Post-Industrial Society) (Paris: Denoel, 1969).
16. ILO, op. cit. pp. 70–5.
17. 'Wages and Working Conditions in Multinational Enterprises' (Geneva: ILO 1976).
18. 'Budget Financing and Monetary Control', Monetary Studies Series (Paris: OECD, 1982).
19. World Development Report, OECD, 1982.
20. G. K. Helleiner, *Intra-firm Trade and the Developing Countries* (London: Macmillan, 1981), pp. 10–11.
21. *Transnational Corporations in World Development: A Re-examination* (New York: United Nations, 20 March 1978), p. 43.
22. Helleiner, op. cit., p. 10.
23. UN, op. cit., p. 44.
24. M. Ghertman, 'Choix d'une monnaie de facturation et gestion du risque de change' (Choice of Billing Currency and Management of Exchange Risk), *Banque*, no. 373 (May 1978), pp. 595–603, and no. 374 (June 1978), pp. 739–49.
25. In 1982 (the regulations can change from year to year).
26. J. Baranson, *Industrial Technologies for Developing Economies* (London: Pall Mall Press, 1969).

27. G. Hufbauer and F. Adler, *Overseas Manufacturing Investment and the Balance of Payments*, US Treasury, 1968; and W. Reddeway, *Effects of UK Direct Investment Overseas* (Cambridge University Press, 1968).
28. R. Gilpin, *US Power and the Multinational Corporation* (New York: Basic Books, 1975).
29. Gilpin, op. cit., p. 197.
30. *Transnational Corporations in World Development: A Re-examination* (New York: United Nations, 20 March 1978), p. 275.
31. Survey of Current Business, United States Department of Commerce, vol. 61 (December 1981), p. 37.
32. Handbook of International Trade and Development Statistics, United Nations, 1979; and Department of Statistics, UNCTAD, for 1980.
33. United Kingdom Balance of Payments figures, CSO.
34. I. Sachs, *Initiations à l'écodéveloppement* (Initiation to Eco-development) (Paris: Privat, coll. Regard, 1981).
35. E. Emmanuel, *Appropriate or Underdeveloped Technology?* (Chichester: Wiley, 1982).
36. G. Maxcy, *The Multinational Motor Industry* (London: Croom Helm, 1981), pp. 127–8 and 264–9.
37. A. Rugman, 'Transfer Pricing Problems and the Multinational Corporations', Chap. 4 in A. R. Negandhi (ed.), *Functioning of the Multinational Corporation* (New York: Pergamon Press, 1980), pp. 51–73.
38. S. Lall, 'Transfer Pricing by Multinational Manufacturing Firms', *Oxford Bulletin of Economics and Statistics* (August 1975), pp. 173–95; and C. Vaitsos, *Intercountry Income distribution and Transnational Enterprises* (Oxford University Press, 1974).
39. R. Lattes, *Mille milliards de dollars* (One Trillion Dollars) (Paris: J. C. Lattes, 1982), p. 30.

CHAPTER 4: MULTINATIONALS AND SOCIETY

1. For detailed information on these conditions, which vary from host country to host country, the reader can consult: Business International, *Investing, Licensing and Trading Conditions Abroad*, Geneva, 12–14 Chemin Rieu; updated twice yearly.
2. Conference organized in Paris by the *International Herald Tribune* on 8–9 February 1982.
3. R. Lattes, *Mille milliards de dollars* (One Trillion Dollars) (Paris: J. C. Lattes, 1982), p. 35.
4. United Nations Department of Economic and Social Affairs, 'The Impact of Multinational Corporations on Development and on International Relations', Report of the Group of Eminent Persons, E.74.11.A.5. (New York: UN, 1974), statement by Professor Edith Penrose, p. 149.
5. US Senate Committee on Foreign Relations, *Multinational Corporations and United States Foreign Policy*, 'Hearings before the Subcom-

mittee on Multinational Corporations of the Committee of Foreign Relations, United States Senate, 93rd Congress on the International Telephone and Telegraph Company and Chile, 1970–71', 20, 21, 22, 27, 28, 29 March and 2 April 1973 (Washington: US Government Printing Office, 95–709 O., 1973), pp. 93–125, 277–318, 457–515.

6. In 'Professionalism: lessons from Chile', in *Medicine in Society*, vol. 7, nos 2 & 3, pp. 14–19 and no. 4, pp. 30–3, Geoffrey Hamilton describes thoroughly the role of the Chilean doctors in Allende's fall.

7. International Chamber of Commerce, 'Guidelines for International Investment', 29 November 1972.

8. OECD, *The OECD Guidelines for Multinational Enterprises*, Declaration on International Investment and Multinational Enterprises, 21 June 1976.

9. ILO, *The Tripartite Declaration of Principles concerning Multinational Enterprises and Social Policy*, 1977.

10. ICFTU, *The Multinational Charter*, Mexico, 17–25 October 1975.

11. WHO, *Infant Formula Marketing Code*, Geneva, 20 May 1981.

12. *Le Monde*, 23 March 1982, p. 45.

13. A. Touraine, Z. Hegedus, F. Dubet and M. Wieviorka, *Prophétie anti-nucléaire* (Anti-Nuclear Prophecy) (Paris: Le Seuil, 1980).

14. P. Simmonot, *Les nucléocrates* (The Nucleocrats) (Paris: PUF, 1978).

15. J. P. Vignolle, 'Mélange des genres, alchimie sociale: la production des disques de variétés' (Mixture of Types, Social Alchemy: the Production of Pop Records), *Sociologie du Travail*, no. 2/80, Paris, pp. 129–51.

16. W. W. Rostow, *The Stages of Economic Growth, a Non-Communist Manifesto* (Cambridge: University Press, 1960), pp. 4–16.

17. Work of Prebisch and Singer at ECLA (Economic Commission for Latin America, United Nations). See A. Pinto, *America Latina: el pensamiento de la CEPAL* (Latin America: ECLA Views) (Santiago: Editorial Universitaria, 1969).

18. A. Emmanuel, *L'Echange inégal* (The Unequal Exchange) (Paris: Maspero, Coll. Economie et Socialisme, 1972).

19. Gunder Frank, 'Latinoamerica: subdesarrollo capitalista o revolucion socialista' (Latin America: Capitalist Underdevelopment or Socialist Revolution), *Pensamiento Critico* 13 (1968).

20. R. M. Martini, *Subdesarrollo y revolucion* (Underdevelopment and Revolution) (Mexico: Singlo XXI, 1969).

21. R. Dumont and M. F. Mottin, *Le mal-développement en Amérique Latine* (Wrong-Development in Latin America) (Paris: Le Seuil, 1981).

22. J. Serra and F. Cardoso, 'Les mésaventures de la dialectique de la dépendence' (The Misadventures of the Dialectics of Dependence), *Amérique Latine*, no. 1 (January–March 1981), CETRAL, Paris, pp. 25–44.

23. J. L. Reiffers, *Sociétés transnationales et développement endogène* (Transnational Corporations and Endogenous Development) (Paris: Les Presses de l'UNESCO, 1981).

Index

Entries consisting of initials or acronyms are grouped at the beginning of their respective initial letters.

Distribution by subsidiaries, 10
Driver and Vehicle Licensing
 Centre (DVLC), 81
Dunlop, 13

ENI, 21
Eastern European countries,
 subsidiaries developing in, 13
Economic development, 123
 role of multinationals, 82–8
 theory of dependence, 116
 theory of stages, 116
Economic policies, 123
 national, 90
Eisenhower, Dwight D., 21
Electronic equipment, 13
 companies in top fifty
  multinationals, 59–60
 technology transfer, 84
Elf-Erap, 21, 95
Employment, 122
 by governments, 90, 94
 by multinationals, 94: compared
  with total in employment,
  52, 65–6; developed and
  developing countries
  compared, 66; in country of
  origin, 68
 by state-controlled companies,
  94
 statistics, 91
 terms of, 103
 see also Labour
Energy sources, research by
 multinationals, 23
 see also Petroleum industry
Esso, *see* Exxon
European Confederation of Trade
 Unions (ECTU), 110
European Economic Community
 (EEC)
 effect of US multinationals, 9
 influence on multinationals'
  structure in UK, 56
 internal trade, 10
 sales of US automobiles, 28
 as single market, 9
 UK entry, and subsequent US
  investment, 49

European multinationals, 121
 automobile companies, 25:
  in Latin America, 29
 companies in top fifty, 60
 concessions in oil producing
  countries, 17
 development, 10–16
 early formation, 7
 growth of investment, 11–12, 15
 in US, 11
Exchange rates, 74, 123
 economic effect of fluctuations,
  75
 effect of cash management
  practices, 78–9
 effect of devaluation by one
  country, 75
 effect of multinational
  operations, 75, 76–9
 influenced by interest rates, 78
Exxon, 20, 21
 economic importance, 45, 48

Factoring arrangements, by
 Dunlop, 13
Fast food industry, 114
Fiat, 25, 29
Food industry
 companies in top fifty
  multinationals, 59–60
 cultural factors, 114
Ford, 52, 58
 development, 25–6
 operations in India, 86
 overseas output (1939), 27
 pre-war German restrictions, 27
Foreign exchange controls, 77,
 94-5
France
 banking, 31–2
 concentration in automobile
  industry, 58
 control of multinationals'
  operations, 95
 defence equipment for India, 86
 development of oil industry, 20
 employment, 92: in government
  service, 91; growth in
  ·overseas divisions, 69